ONE

Face to face contact

Experiencing ET consciousness

And human consciousness evolution

Yossi Ronen

Dedication

In loving memory of my father

Rafael Ronen

Copyright © 2020 by Yossi Ronen
Cover Produced by Yossi Ronen
Editing by Desta Barnabe and Adele Barnabe
Interior Design and Layout by Desta Barnabe
Special thanks to Pia Rosenbach for the final linguistic editing

First Printing August 2020
ISBN: 9798680016749

WEBSITE: WWW.ONEYOSSIRONEN.COM
YOUTUBE: www.youtube.com/user/YOSSIRONEN
MAIL: YOSRON7@GMAIL.COM

Contents

Introduction

The first part of this book covers my testimony concerning my face-to-face encounter and direct communication with several extraterrestrials, intelligent beings, whom I refer to as 'the visitors'. This encounter occurred in 1981 when I lived in L.A. for about one year.

The very appearance of these beings that stood before me was a complete contradiction to anything I had ever known about everyday reality as I recognize it. Following this encounter, at the young age of 21 years old, the course of my entire life has changed, and since that day, the meaning of this experience has become an integral part of my life.

After many testimonials we have heard from other experiencers who have also met with the visitors, we know now that the visitors' communication with us goes straight into our consciousness.

In my case, the communication had another aspect to it. The contact showed itself to me in two different states of my consciousness; one as part of an out-of-body experience, and the other when I was awake and fully conscious in front of them, face to face.

To this day, I cannot clearly say whether the visitors planned to communicate with me in both ways, or if it was unexpected. In any case, meeting and interacting with the visitors in both states allowed me to understand more about the consciousness aspects in which this very different, but not separate ways of communication occurs between us.

Composing this book has taken many years. It was difficult at first, to come to terms with the actual encounter or even to discuss it. Then to comprehend the complexity of the experience I had to translate the nonverbal communication into spoken language and rational terms and phrases, and at last, the repeated self-examination I did for my understanding and interpretation.

The visitors have a different perception of reality compared to our own. I had to attempt and grasp their mode of thinking.

Sharing the visitors' consciousness during my contact with them allowed me briefly to experience the way they see us and their understanding of us.

In this book, I summarize my perspective of my encounter and its implications.

Hopefully, this writing will assist us all in our joint endeavor to better understand this new reality we are currently facing, having realized that we are not alone.

In April 1981, I came to live and work with my brother, who had already been living in the Valley of Los Angeles. As I turned 21 years old that year, I longed to cover new grounds and to save up for college once I got back home. We lived in a two-bedroom condo, where my bed was situated at the far end of the living room.

One

First Contact through two states of consciousness

It happened on the evening of a sunny day. My brother and I came home to rest after a long working day. My brother was sleeping in his room, and I was dozing off, facing the wall beside my bed. After a few moments, I shut my eyes and for the first time in my life, found myself within a dream that was taking place outside my body, in that very room.

In my dream, I knew I was outside my body, which was sleeping in bed.

I didn't have an actual body, but it was perhaps something akin to a child's small body, transparent, without any definite outlines.

I felt happy being close to the bed, hovering over it, then sitting at the nearby table, looking around, at peace, fully conscious and aware of what was going on. I was smiling, whilst looking/watching, at my sleeping body.

The sensation of the distance from my body felt pleasant, liberating, free, and light. It was a good feeling. I was seeing, sensing, smelling, and hearing everything that was going on around me without the familiar boundaries of my body. My brother was sound asleep in the next room, on the other side of the wall, breathing calmly.

And then, I saw them! They were in the room as well, they were not quite human, little entities between the armchair and the couch, by the TV. One of them was standing by my sleeping body, watching it.

Amused, I looked at them, watched them wobble along in a funny, clumsy way across the room from one spot to another. They were looking around the apartment with such curiosity and wonder. One of them picked up a piece of paper, very carefully, as though seeing it for the first time. He touched it and felt it, clasped his fingers around it, listened for the sound of crumpling paper, smelled it. They looked similar to human children in a new playground. I felt I knew them like they were childhood friends of mine.

They were a little under four feet, three inches tall. Their heads were slightly bigger than ours. I do not recall how many fingers they had. I think I saw five in each hand, longer than our own, gentle and supple. One of the 'guests' was chubby, his belly protruding over his scrawny legs. His walk was also clumsier than that of the others. Another was so skinny I could see the outline of his bones right under his skin.

I was watching them calmly and blissfully. We were all rejoicing together. One of them was moving back and forth across the mat, wobbling like a duck, marveling and laughing like a child taking his very first steps. The more solemn among the guests was concentrating on my sleeping body over the bed, watching it closely, focusing on my head, which was resting on the pillow. It seemed he was communicating with my body, perhaps trying to help with something...

I remember that at the end of the dream, when I was about to return to my body, I was laughing along with them, wholehearted laughter of understanding, acceptance, and love for one another. Vaguely, I recalled that this laughter we all shared had some reason to it, we shared something meaningful together, something loving and pleasant. Perhaps we were laughing at the human confusion and the fear these types of meetings often bring about.

Upon awakening I was still smiling, recalling the weird dream.

I wondered about this unfamiliar expanse my imagination had brought forth, complete with such a palpable dream, which was so strange and wild.

Suddenly, I heard these strange sounds coming from inside the room I was in, like bare feet making rapid steps across the carpet. I rubbed my eyes, still in bed, facing the wall. There was a rustle of things being moved about, crumpling paper, strange whispers. My smile was gone, my heart pounding. *'Did thieves' brake into our house? Are they trying to keep quiet so I don't wake up?'*

I remembered I had locked the door from the inside. *'Impossible. No one could possibly have gotten in.'*

Turning around to face the room, I felt an electric shock hit me hard and I began to tremble helplessly. Right across from me, less than two feet away, stood one of the visitors from the dream I just had. He was staring right at me.

Four or five others were standing right behind him.

His huge eyes looked deep into me. They were black and shiny, like pupils that had grown to a huge size. I felt small as if he was observing me under a microscope.

Then, I felt a terrible fear. It was strong and unfamiliar. Curling up, I gasped. My breath stopped. I tried to digest the fact that I was looking at the same visitors that I had just seen in my dream.

What was I was seeing? *'Is this still the dream or did I wake up?'* I shook my head, pinched my hand and the pain made me realize I was awake. *'Am I out of my mind? What's going on? What's happening to me?'*

The visitor's gaze went right through me with such force, such an immense, paralyzing effect. Fear was rapidly surging within me. My muscles contracted so hard; I couldn't move. *'Something strange and out of this world, scary is invading my insides now.'* It felt so frightening to be under someone else's control, another person who dominated me, who could have me act however he pleased. I felt this danger as if I had only a few more moments before I would be taken up by something so much bigger than me. *'It was like he was about to swallow me.'*

'They are not of this world.' That much was obvious to me. Their curious bodies had these bright green and

orange-rust colored patches. Their skin had grooves, and yet, it was gentle and soft, hairless… In relation to their small bodies, their heads were big and their eyes were black, elliptical, with no eyelids. They were so big that they took up most of their face. They had two tiny slits for a nose, a very narrow groove for a mouth, no lips, and a small chin. The sight of them before my very eyes was so shocking, it felt like my own end, like ceasing to be, like death.

My guest wasn't speaking to me, but something inside me knew he was seeing and experiencing everything I was feeling and thinking like I was an open book to him. In my paralysis, I saw my own fear and helplessness reflected through his black, shiny eyes.

He was experiencing my pain as though it was his own, and I knew this experience was unfamiliar to him. I felt how, for the very first time, they experienced human fear. I felt him worrying, wanting me to keep calm, and at the same time, doing nothing. I was merely holding on, suffering my own fear of death, I was screaming inside my own head, *'Enough already, run, RUN!'*

The guest just kept standing there, right next to me. I was sitting there, frozen. It felt like they were drilling into my mind. *'Why am I paralyzed with fear? Why are* they taking control over me, penetrating my every thought? What do they want from me?'

I recalled the pleasant dream I just woke up from. *'It's them. They were really there. So, what was happening? It wasn't really a dream? A short while ago I knew them and it was all fine, without this fear...'* For one brief moment, I was able to stop this trembling all over, this terrible fear for my life. With my very last ounce of strength, in my desperation, and perhaps because I had no other choice, I tried to look beyond my fear, to regard them as something else other than what I saw. In some hopeful attitude, unrelated to my own body, still petrified and anxious, I was looking into his eyes, searching for that love I remembered from the dream.

The pain from the sound of the drilling that I kept hearing, as though it was forcing its way right through me all this time, began slowing down. As it adjusted its pace, it began to sound different, clearer, more intelligible. *'Are these their thoughts? Their emotions?'*

The noise slowly diminished, and I began noticing more sensations, more thoughts. *'Is this their communication that I'm hearing? Is this what I am sensing?'*

And it was at that precise moment, that I began experiencing them with my own consciousness. All at once, the full awareness of one of the beings before me flowed into me, and through him, via him, that of all the others too. The sight of their faces did not change, but everything the guests were thinking or sensing passed on to me too, and was now inside me, expanding, as if it were my own consciousness. Their thoughts did not consist of definite words. Rather, this was a wide expanse, a multifaceted, flow of consciousness that had the feeling of an enormously huge event. They were experiencing a simple peace I was not familiar with. It had no sense of superiority, as one would expect given their formidable power.

The guests' consciousness was like an open book to me. I felt them completely: pleasant, still, lucid, and clear. Their thoughts and emotions seemed harmonious, unified, unseparated.

I encountered their love and acceptance toward me as well, and not thanks to anything about me. Likewise, they simply accepted themselves and each other unconditionally, endlessly. They were transparent, upfront, and self-conscious, as well as toward one another, without any need to hide, playact, repress, or be anything else other than what they were precisely at that moment. I felt they loved themselves and accepted themselves at face value, without any judgment, good or bad, and that was the same way they treated whatever was around them, their own kind, any human beings, or anything else whatsoever…

This feeling reminded me of something from my distant past, so distant, I even forgot I had missed it. It was innocence, pure, childlike innocence…

The fear I was sensing abated somewhat, and I opened up to the guest before me a bit more. He felt this, and his openness toward me got so intense, his entire being was given unto me, to have as my own. Then, I was experiencing his thoughts, sensing his own emotions, his self, his consciousness, spreading, unbounded, limitless, beyond the confines of definitions. It was such a pleasant sensation I can barely describe it.

'He is aware of any speck of matter inside this room and beyond, of any point in time and place, far above and beyond my comprehension.'

For the first time in my life, I sensed my own self via their consciousness, from a different perspective; I saw me, the expanses of my own awareness, through them. Together with them and via their perception, my own understanding too was experiencing and spreading in any direction in time, to the past and the future wide and full of possibilities. Clearly, this capacity of expanding consciousness that I felt was something any person could have.

We encountered each other in a completely different way than the way we humans understand one another and reality in general. There were no boundaries, no form of separation between us. I saw what each and every one of them saw, just as I was seeing it for myself. We shared consciousness; each of the visitors was experiencing the whole of us, and at the same time, each and every one of us had a consciousness of his own, personal, clear, distinct, and unique unto itself. In some wondrous way, we were also aware of belonging to the whole. The physical distance between us had become symbolic and distinguishing, but not a separation.

I came into contact with infinite contents through the connection we built. Wanting to know more about them, I asked a question, "Are you from another planet?" My question made them laugh, but their laughter was not a sound.

Then, all at once, I received a reply right into me, like a surprising understanding with no beginning and end.

They answered me without the words that make up human thought. It was far from the way we humans think or speak. It was as if, through one injection into me, I received a whole content that, were I to translate it into my own words, would run as follows;

"Well, 'another planet' is the logical place according to your reasoning. For you, this is the most suitable translation for what you are experiencing – that we came from a different place, far away ... in your language, you might say that we came from another dimension."

I allowed myself to open up to them, without thought, without fear and without being disturbed by their presence within me, the space they occupied in me. At that moment, I felt the attention of everyone in the room turned to me in full. Joy and immense love broke forth and flowed from them to every cell in my body.

More and more they felt like some part of me. They now knew me as they experienced a dormant part of them that had awakened, awakened unto itself and thus to the reality around it, expanding as light spreads, touches, and illuminates some other place. I was now connected to a vast, radiant essence.

Vibrations of acceptance and love were now reverberating between us. My complete merger with them, starting with my own familiar self, was now spreading far beyond, to experience another presence now. It was the presence of some tremendous love that transcended the guests themselves. Its source was different, incomprehensible to me. It was a love that illuminated something within me, evoking something forgotten. A torrent of bliss flowed through me like water.

Now, I was becoming aware of a place in my own body that had always contained something akin to infinite light, some sort of immense power and love whose origin was beyond my comprehension, as well as beyond the grasp of the visitors.

I tried to track the source of this light, that I was experiencing in every cell and fiber of my body and mind. This appeared to be the foundation of my being and my consciousness, of everything I was aware of. In fact, it held, sustained, and realized my very existence. It was clear to me that this was also the very source of life itself, and that it had contained within it the whole of existence and of reality, and that this is the very "light" everything consists of. For the visitors, apparently, their constant awareness of it was the reason for their sense of security, peace, and happiness, and in those moments, mine too.

Within a split second, I saw images of my life's memories and thoughts from that moment back in time – all the way to my early childhood. This light has always been there. It was the very source and the very force that enabled my life - and reality as a whole.

Also, the pain, the hardship, the suffering, and the evil, that I had witnessed and experienced throughout my life until then, also stemmed from the same light that sustains and loves.

That love has always been the existential basis for everything that has happened. A sense of calm and comfort overwhelmed me as I realized that everything that had happened or would ever happen in the future was and is an act of that same tremendous light and love.

The visitors were aware of this with their entire being, and they had always been grateful, sensing the love for that one light that encompasses and sustains everything. They were happy to have received the right to experience the interaction with this light simply and continuously, happy to be connected to it and to have dedicated themselves to it. In some natural, simple way, they are aware that it sustains them, that it is not separate from them and that nevertheless, it also exceeds them. They are aware of their place within it and wish what it wishes.

Passionate at the bliss of experiencing this light, I wanted to see and understand more and more. I asked them without words, "What is this light? Is this God? Is this the source of our reality? So, what is it? I wish to understand more, what lays beyond it? What supersedes it and contains it?"

All that I received by way of reply was silence, a barrier. I got no response, no perception, no insight into any of these questions.

There was a sense of some sudden shock emanating from the visitors towards me, as well as a deep sense of concern for me.

It seems that they did not expect me to try to understand, to get my mind around the source of light, something that the encounter with them allowed me to experience in full for the first time in my life.

At that moment, I realized that the guests themselves do not attempt to understand this light. Beyond the fact that they were experiencing its love, they did not need to comprehend it in the rational, human way that I am trying to grasp now, especially in my conscious and awake state, through my body as well.

In my enthusiasm to know and understand more, thanks to the encounter with them, my curiosity sought to identify that which lay beyond the limits of my capacity.

Something akin to a shock shuddered inside me. This was the contact with the very limitations of my consciousness and perception, however great during those moments of my connection with them.

At the same moment, I felt the fear creeping back again until it quickly overshadowed the fear of what was now occurring right before me. The guests were beginning to sever the connection that had formed between us to protect me.

However palpable the experience of being at one with them was, but for a short while just then, a sense clearer and more tangible than anything I had ever experienced in my life arose in me. Once again, I reverted to the realization of the irrationality of what was happening, that this experience made no sense. Perhaps what I was seeing was actually some hallucination which I was imagining to be some sort of reality, and that perhaps, maybe irrevocably, I had already 'lost it' altogether.

The immense, loving light I had felt only a moment earlier had disappeared from my consciousness, chased away, as it were, by the fear that had returned to me in full force and was now separating us, standing between me and the light. It whisked it away to such an extent, that is was as though that light had never existed. My sense of security and love was gone, and much like a cloud blocks the sunlight, a foreboding dark shadow was cast over me.

The appearance of the guests before me now seemed like doors that had flung open too suddenly and too forcibly for my simple life. My familiar, steady ground, that I have always counted on for support, suddenly burst open, forcing me to fall and lose myself in some unknown abyss. This fear made my heart beat so fast, I could hear the blood flow in my ears like a train whistling as it rushes in, on the verge of colliding with me. I felt my body's fear through them as well. They were experiencing it too, and I knew that fearing death was an unfamiliar experience for them, not as we know it.

The experience of the encounter was already well beyond my powers, and I felt that my body was no longer capable of sustaining its toll. My guests, who had known and who had felt every cell in my body, seemed beside themselves with concern. Sadly, I realize were about to leave the room and disappear from sight.

They imparted one quick message, a lightning-like flash, before leaving me be.

I received their message via the guest nearest to me, who looked at me with his eyes and passed it on to me in a more familiar, human way.

He relayed right into my conscious mind a series of images that looked like a movie, a movie featuring me, a movie I was watching from within it.

I saw myself in this large field of green grass and trees, on a pleasant day. I felt the fertile soil alive and nourishing the grass and the trees. The whole vegetation was vibrating along with the light of the sun and the pure air, which was bursting, full, pleasant, and fragrant. High above it all was the canopy of the firmament, clear and blue. Cows roamed the grass, keeping close to one another, grazing slowly and calmly, relishing the grass.

Suddenly, without so much as a warning, a deafening roar came over, rolling as it drew closer. A huge fire was bursting over the tall treetops from afar. Red and yellow tongue-like flames covered the whole horizon, rushing, roaring, and consuming everything, engulfing all with such fury. The cows, the grass, and the green trees all turned to black, dead ashes.

A deep sense of anguish swept over me.

The pain I felt while seeing these pictures mainly came through the cow's eyes a second before being burned; they looked straight at me.

Through their eyes, they spoke straight into my heart, "Why don't you see us?" Sudden heat, the burn in my frozen heart. Suddenly, I was paying attention to the innocence and purity of those cows, whose whole being was only giving- their milk, their bodies, and their children. Through their innocent, loving eyes, they were not angry and blaming me, they simply did not understand why I don't see. Then I saw everything, the burnt trees, the burnt air, the black grass, the blackened sky, my body and mind blockage. Only then did I realize how much my arrogance as a human being convinced me that I was in control of everything that was going on around me, that I was the person who already thinks he knows and understands everything, even the nature that gives birth and revives me every moment and with every breath.

I felt we were granted the freedom to do what we wanted here and then burned the house we were given.

'This was my home, it was under my care, and now it was completely burned.' The destruction I saw was a warning, a cautionary tale in the form of the image of desolation for us humans, as well as a warning for us – the sight of my/ our, irresponsibility, the sight of the immense potential and tremendous capacity we have for self-destruction, of all the world around us.

And thus, ended those images the guests communicated to me.

I was now feeling their suffering, resulting from their consciousness connecting with mine, and thus with my suffering, my fear. *'They are going away from me now in order to free themselves.'*

They moved away from me to the edge of the room, huddling together, holding hands, and started moving in a spinning circle. As their rotation accelerated, they changed and became more and more transparent. The outline of their bodies began to blur and fade as the circle they had formed got smaller and smaller inward, towards its center, until a bright, uniform white light appeared where they had just been, a circle of light spinning at a tremendous speed, then shrinking into this tiny point of light until it too disappeared.

Yossi Ronen

Two

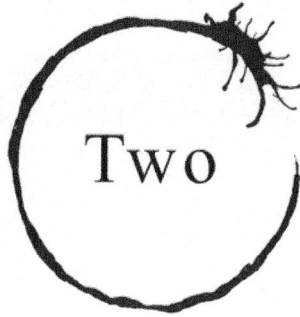

After the Encounter, The Impact on the Body and Mind

The room was empty now. I let out a scream, still sitting up in bed. My body and I were in a state of shock, bliss, terror, and amazement.

My brother, who was sleeping in the next room, was awakened by my scream and rushed over to my side, asking me, all concerned, what was the matter.

I could not bring myself to answer him. I accidentally let out a scream, I wasn't able to hold it in. This suddenly released from my body that was petrified and breathless, paralyzed with fear.

After taking a few deep breaths, and mumbling faintly, I forced myself to gesture that nothing was the matter. My brother handed me a glass of water and returned to his room. From his face, I could tell that he was quite worried.

Getting out of bed, I stepped into our yard. Slowly, I sat down on a chair right by the door and breathed in the evening air. A pleasant, quiet breeze carried the scent of the ocean in, cooling my face.

I still felt shaken up in spite of this inner bliss, all of this was as incomprehensible as it was alien. What I just witnessed was a sudden invasion of my normal life, there was a mixture of worry and turmoil, and these thoughts flooded into my head. There was also a feeling of underlying happiness and a new-found, clear sense of security, that was nevertheless very abstract, devoid of any clear rationale or logic.

The thought that I had suddenly become aware of new expanses of existence through this encounter with tiny guests who had come over from a different dimension also reeked of a profound lack of any sense of reality.

I resolved to tell no one what had occurred.

In my weary and anguished state, I looked down. My eyes filled with tears at the prospect of my strange future; I must be losing it. It seemed as if I was going mad…

My eyes rested on my hands, which lay on my knees. They seemed different somehow, through my tears. Same hands, same familiar fingers, but they now had thin red lines. Terrified, I quickly wiped my tears away and took another look. Up close, I realized that these red lines were my capillaries, running along the back of my hand.

'What does it mean? This cannot be a hallucination. I'm not dreaming. And yet, I am seeing something that cannot be seen.'

Gently, I touched the outer layer of my skin, right over the blood vessels I was seeing. *'If I imagine this, I am about to find out for sure now.'* But no, I could still see them.

I felt my fingers, feeling their way on the back of my hand. I could see my capillaries moving along with the skin under my fingers. *'This is for real.'* Strangely, I was also sensing my blood flowing through my blood vessels as I watched my hands. I saw my blood flow.

This surprising sight had given me such pause, I was not concerned for my sanity. My consciousness is different now. My senses seemed to pick up far more than they usually did. My eyes noticed things I had never seen up to now. It suddenly dawned on me I could see very closely as if I was looking through a magnifying glass. I also noticed I could see from a greater distance, further too, regardless if I had my glasses on or not.

My hearing was also more acute. Sounds coming from afar I was able to hear quite effortlessly, even sounds I had never heard before. My nose suddenly picked up all sorts of new scents and smells, too.

I tried to figure out what it was about me that had changed. Certainly, I was still under the influence of the encounter, but the visitors had gone. Something within my body, the behavior of my senses, had changed.

Looking at the tree near the entrance to our condominium, I could see the movement of the leaves rustling gently in the quiet breeze.

'Was I hearing the sight of the leaves?'

Looking around, everything I was seeing also had its own distinct rich sound, enhancing the site.

My senses converged, working in unison, in some mutual, joint consciousness, that allowed each sense to experience so much more. My vision and my hearing seemed to have merged, so in some way, I was able to see what I was hearing and hear what I was seeing. I felt my sight so much more now.

The sights and sounds had particular scents and emotions, which in turn helped me in noticing each in a more defined, more distinct way than I was used to. I kept checking and rechecking what I was sensing. Unable to stop doubting what was going on, I had to examine my senses to be sure I wasn't imagining some strange phenomenon. I went over to the other side of our building to see for myself if I really was smelling or feeling the actual cat that was walking there.

I dug a few inches under the earth by my chair in our yard just to see if there really was this ant, whose distress I seemed to feel, or see, or hear.

Coupled with my bewilderment and second-guessing concerning what had happened, I was excited by this wonderful sense of openness about reality in my body and mind.

I felt within my body such expanses of unfamiliar freedom, the absence of those boundaries that have always boxed me in.

One of our neighbors walked in, saying hello as he passed me by on the way to his apartment door. I found myself swept away by this new burst of the mental experience of this person who had come by. We've been neighbors for a few months now. He was an average guy, nothing unusual about him… but this time, I was taken aback by the huge experience of coming across him, as a human being. I could see how he had this inner space the like of which I had never seen, that his essence was so lovely and pleasant, that he had this unfamiliar degree of love he wasn't even aware of, a love that reverberated through each fiber of his being and soul.

I nodded back to echo his hello, but I could not bring myself to utter a syllable.

He walked to his apartment, leaving behind a trail of that beautiful, energetic essence, like a pleasant scent that is slow to fade. I was glad at this, for through him I had come to know for the first time, about the wonderful essence of all people. Nevertheless, I was also saddened at his obvious ignorance about this, that we humans were unaware of it. We do not see our real selves or each other.

Somehow, I knew this new-found physical ability would soon dissipate, and therefore, that the freedom to experience this vast expanse of reality could turn into some faded memory, at best...

I felt a strong need to grasp this experience, get my head around it, and retain it. I wanted to understand what had changed, what was going on in my body, in my mind, and my consciousness right now, perhaps to learn how it worked, preserve it in my memory so that I might repeat it.

It was clear to me that the guests had given me no supernatural ability of any kind. Something about the encounter with them had awakened this unknown thing within me, between myself and I, perhaps physically in my brain or mind, that changed my consciousness. I knew this ability was natural, even basic. Something which I as a part of the whole of mankind had always had.

I took a few deep breaths until my body was calm, and wiped my tears of bliss and embarrassment away.

Looking around, I still saw the same houses, bushes, and trees, but I was seeing them differently. What was it in my consciousness that had changed? It was a follow up to something that went on in my mind or brain during the meeting with the visitors, something whose impact lingered still. I knew it was related to the experience of that deep connection between and with them.

However individually different each of us was in the contact, there was nevertheless something connecting us all, this one thing we had all experienced together, a state in which each of us continued to be distinct from one another and yet, at the same time, joined to the very source of light, akin to this deep love that connected us all, thereby comprising everyone's consciousness. Therefore, the awareness of each of us also comprised that of the others- each part also contained the whole.

This way of connection between the distinct persons was now also physically taking place in my body function, maybe in my brain, between my different senses, and the objective world reality.

Together with the regular sights around me, I was also aware of some other additional essence, an almost invisible light. It quivered, brightly, almost yellow, gentle, calming, emanating from anything my eyes rested upon. This light shone from the bushes, the trees, all the greenery, from the ground, from the walls of the houses... It was the same light wherever I looked, one light, and yet, it erupted in some unique way from everything around me.

Searching for the source of this light, I realized this was beyond my reach. It was beginning to be tangible, and when it appeared to me, it was carried by the light of the sun. It was one with the sun, shining on everything and was reflected from them and through them. This light also had a peaceful, calming yet undefined sound, as though it was comprised of different sounds that merged harmoniously, sounding much like the sound of running water in a tranquil brook.

When the light was reflected off the various things all around me, something about it changed and took on a unique essence through them, as though it was speaking through it and becoming this object's unique language.

Each light reaching upwards from the bush next to me also had this sort of sound, emotion, and scent that was unique to it. The light flowed in this new language through the bush. It appeared that this essence that was in everything was also the same essence that had always connected everything. There was also this emotion in it, in which I could identify love.

The simple unity I had experienced with the guests, was now highlighting within me, the possibility of paying attention to this unity I was now seeing all around me. It was as though this experience had thawed something that was frozen in my psyche, and now it was flowing and connecting various things and places, allowing me to feel love for no reason, highlighting the reality of that invisible love that exists unconditionally, all the time, everywhere.

In my regular state, every object around me seemed separate from the other; the tree is distinct, apart from the ground, and likewise, air, sun, and so on... but now, as some resonance to the experience of sharing all my different senses jointly, I was seeing the same connection that had always been there, all around. Now, the trees are a clear continuation of the ground below and of the sun and the air above, without any intermission or pause between any of them, like one continuous body.

The trees were nourished by the earth. The food and the water that nourished it flowed through the trees as well, so they were, in fact, a direct continuation of the ground. Sunlight descended and permeated the leaves, merged with the water, and became part of the plant. The tree was also the condensation of the sunlight; light flowed through the leaves downwards, descending right into the heart of the earth along with the roots and making it fertile. One complete cycle of life traveled from the ground below to the sun above and back down again. Sunlight met the earth and the water in each leaf, where they connected, as though making love with one another. Fire and water converged into one, giving life in the process.

I looked at the tree leaves right in front of me.

Then I went deeper into feeling the sensation of the leaves at the top of the tree which faced upwards to the blue sky, and for the first time ever, noticed something else; the tree was conscious and in a deep, continuing state of thankfulness for its existence, and for the light, he was receiving.

Three

One Day After the Encounter

The next day, most of the physical signs of the encounter which had appeared right after it was gone. No external sign lingered, either. That sublime consciousness that had opened up within me was declining.

Back then, there was no way to publicly report this event, nor were there groups of people discussing their experiences with extraterrestrials. If there was such a thing during those years, I certainly never heard of it. Back in 1981, there was no internet; I felt completely alone with this experience.

It was no longer easy to continue with my life as usual. Something had happened to me. The experience of the encounter stayed within me, fully palpable, and very present. It was a living memory, clearer than anything I had ever felt. Nevertheless, with each passing day, everyday reality clashed ever more forcibly with the experience of the meeting. The existential meaning that had steered my life since childhood clashed, almost violently, with what I had witnessed and experienced during that encounter, and the different possibilities that arose from it.

'Innocent little aliens? Light? Love? G-d? Everything is One? Where is all that now? Why don't they come and show themselves openly? Why hasn't any physical trace of the encounter lingered? Where did all this beauty that I had seen after the encounter go?'

I told no one about my experience. *'Stop trying to figure out what happened,'* I kept telling myself; it was much bigger than me. Besides, I wanted to continue with my life as normal, as though nothing had happened.

After about a month, it felt that the inner conflict I was grappling with would not dissipate, but ran much deeper than I could have imagined. The road I had always followed fell apart in view of the meeting. Everything I had seen in the contact, and the new perspective I gleaned, was not rational. I didn't dare to speak about it with anyone. My encounter became a source of distress I was finding increasingly difficult to cope with. With every ounce of strength, I could muster, I kept trying to forget and bury it.

Leaving the U.S., I returned to my childhood home, where my parents were still living. I kept denying the encounter, with even greater insistence. I also abandoned my pursuit of art and painting, which I had once begun with a great passion. Instead, most of my time and energy went into studying electronics, which I had earlier developed an interest in. My rationale was that I needed a steadier and more stable occupation than painting, which is based on one's creative imagination.

Wanting to build myself a new life, the kind that would be more ordinary and commonplace, I finished school, graduated, and got a job at an electronics company. There were good prospects and my chances of advancement were promising.

I quickly got used to waking up early to take the company shuttlebus and then return home the same way each evening. It seemed I made the right choice and got my life back on track, back to a sane and reasonable path.

But one evening, I noticed a fellow co-worker looking through the bus window. I wasn't entirely sure whether I had seen him before, but strangely, seeing him felt very familiar. Instantly, I felt a deep sense of sadness;

I pitied him, his pale-face, his gaze that seemed to be fixed on some point out the bus window. He appeared to be dead and alive at the same time.

It took me a while, but I figured out why this made me feel so profoundly anguished by the end of that evening. I got a clear sense of how removed one can get from oneself. The fear of the encounter I had got me so rattled, I realized that I also had driven myself far from whom I had been. The experience had become an integral part of me and until then, I refused to acknowledge it even to myself.

The very next day I resigned. I got an apartment with roommates in Tel Aviv and moved out of my parent's house. I then decided to go to art school and I began taking classes in mysticism and spirituality, a growing interest. I honed my study of these fields partly through my academic art studies, which touched on them, and partly through books and other courses.

Nevertheless, I didn't realize this newly found attraction to the spiritual had anything to do with that incident with the visitors. It didn't even occur to me there might be another meeting sometime, which I would not be able to ignore or bury.

Four

In the Book Store

One evening, I walked into a bookstore in Tel Aviv and passed the New Sellers bookstand. I paused to look at one of the new arrivals and my eyes rested on its cover.

Suddenly, I was overcome with sudden dizziness! The cover featured the portrait of one of the guests I had encountered. Nearly sick, I was on the verge of fainting. Those same big shiny black eyes were staring at me from the cover of the book: *Communion: A True Story* by Whitley Strieber.

The sight of the visitor's face, which was so similar to the ones I had encountered, shook me to the core, all the more so because it was in the middle of such an ordinary, everyday environment. At that moment, it seemed I was about to face them again.

Frantically, I looked for the original date of publication in English, hoping I had seen this cover at some point; thus, it would have been possible that it made its way to my subconscious and I may have *dreamt* I had met them. *'Maybe it was only some figment of my imagination?!'* But the book was first published in the U.S. in 1987, some years after my encounter with the visitors. No chance I could have seen it before meeting them.

The back cover said the book featured numerous accounts of people who had met the guests. I picked it up and proceeded to the checkout. I was still feeling sick as I stepped out into the crowded street. It was a bright summer day. The sun was blinding, and I was overcome by the sense of having to come to terms with the certainty of having met the guests after all. My step was uneasy and my legs felt unsteady.

I went to the beach and found a bench where I could sit and read the book. For the very first time, I learned that many people all over the world have had a similar experience to mine. It hit me that I could no longer pretend that it never happened.

No longer could I escape the notion that I had to share my experience. It was necessary to talk about it.

The first person I told about it was my mother, the person I knew loved me and accepted me more than anyone else.

When I told her about the encounter, I saw the anguish and pity in her loving eyes. As much as she tried to listen without responding, I could tell by how she tilted her head that she wanted to hide her tears.

I waited for her to tell me on her own volition what she felt about it. The next day, she seemed anxious and upset. When I asked her how she felt about what I had told her, she said she was concerned about me, and feared that I was doing drugs while I was in the States, and that "they must have clouded my mind."

This is but one of many reactions I began getting from those I shared my encounter with. Only a few immediately realized what I was talking about, and their eyes lit up.

Sometime after I began talking about the incident with the guests, all those lingering questions, together with the skeptical responses, made me feel lonely and restless again, to say the least.

Meeting those 'little green creatures', coupled with the spiritual meaning this held, was so far removed from any ordinary perception of reality, that I found myself in a state of utter ignorance as to how to connect to the phenomenon of the meeting. I was so perplexed; I began grappling with many questions. This experience with the guests, is there some sort of truth I am supposed to strive to understand? What does it mean about everyday existence? How am I supposed to come to terms with this huge contradiction between the guests' innocence, naivety, that connection with G-d, which is light and love, and everyday life, which is for the most part suffering, pain, loss, evil, lies, disease, war… whereas for them, everything is ONE?'

Powerless to resolve this conflict, and seeking support to make sense of it all, I wondered if I should pursue another solution – to try and receive the help of the visitors themselves.

Five

An attempt at Another Encounter

I decided to try to initiate another face-to-face contact with the visitors.

It was an unsuccessful attempt and involved an unpleasant result, to some extent, even dangerous.

My decision to write about this effort here in the book was not straightforward, mainly because of the misunderstanding and unnecessary fear it may cause. I decided to explain it here because it may help us understand something important about the limitations of meeting face-to-face with the guests, and more generally about our body, mind, and mental readiness to deal with such unfamiliar ground. Understanding these limitations may help us overcome them.

Since the first meeting with the visitors had already occurred, I thought I could invite them to another physical meeting. The fastest and most direct way of communicating with them and asking them to reappear in front of me would be through consciousness.

I sat down on the armchair I used to sit on when I wanted to close my eyes and go deep into a kind of meditation that is beyond the limits of ordinary awareness. This was how I could come into contact with that deep layer of consciousness, the same place through which the visitors communicated with me when they appeared before me during the first physical encounter.

Closing my eyes, I connected myself to the same place, asking them to appear face to face again.

After a few minutes, I began to feel the same familiar sensation from the encounter, their sense of presence. My eyes were still closed, so I didn't know what was happening, but the familiar feeling of fear that I felt during the original contact started to come over me again. I knew this feeling might come back, so I tried to calm it down. Slowly, I began to open my eyes; right in front of me at about three meters, I began to see some undefined figures, still unclear, almost transparent.

In a few seconds, I realized that I really couldn't go through with it. An unpleasant physical feeling flooded me, and my existential fear hit me with such intensity that I began to feel the same paralysis in my body again. Immediately, I closed my eyes and stopped wanting to meet them. A few moments later, as the fear calmed down a bit, I opened my eyes and was glad they were no longer there. My body released itself from the terrible grip of paralysis that had grabbed it again, similar to the beginning of the first encounter.

What was wrong? Why did the fear flood me even though I was ready for it, I knew I had no reason to be afraid of them?

Also, I began to feel strange and intense dizziness that I had never experienced before. The whole room looked like it was going around me; I was sitting in the armchair, but everything around me, the walls, the furniture, the table, windows, they all were moving around faster and faster.

The speed of the rotation increased so much that I could not see clearly, holding on to the armrest of my chair as if I was about to fly out of it. Everything around me turned into brightly colored spots with each other, becoming brighter and brighter with the rotation and some of them already looked like white lines of dazzling light swirling around me.

A growing physical weakness came over me, and a strong feeling of nausea began to creep into my throat. I managed to lift myself from the armchair and walked step by step to the sink. I started vomiting vigorously and uncontrollably until there was nothing left to come out.

Still, I didn't understand what happened to me. It was only after about an hour when the physical weakness peaked that the reason became clear.

My body was unprepared for the encounter, I invited the visitors to come face to face when my body could not tolerate it. I tried to force my body to be in a condition to allow it. My body received a command from my consciousness to adapt to the situation and it had to make a dramatic and rapid change to allow for the meeting. It had to adjust and needed to be clean. My body had to quickly reach a state that would not physically block conscious contact through its senses into the guests' consciousness space, but it was not ready for that. Perhaps one could say that my body's energy frequency at that time could not match the energy frequency of the guests, which was possibly purer and much higher than mine.

My body's automatic response to adjust was to purify itself in any way that was possible. What it did was simple. The body tried to cleanse itself and throw out what it could, everything that could be spent ...

Later, I felt good and light, even pleasant and refined. But my body was very weak. After recovering a little and being able to walk, I went to bed. I awoke after a 12-hour sleep, feeling healthy and fresh.

It was possible that at the first meeting, I was able to withstand the vibration of the visitors because they knew when and how to show up, so I could stand it. The first encounter that they initiated began outside the body, and so it was a much more relaxed and positive experience.

Because of this fear-based intervention, I knew I must prepare myself to deal with both the mental and instinctive physical fear of my body when I was to meet them again, fully conscious, and awake.

Six

The Key: Clinical Death, Meeting the Visitors and Physical Translating of Our Non-Physical Experiences

Our normal waking consciousness, rational consciousness as we call it, is but one special type of consciousness, whilst all about it, parted from it by the filmiest of screens, there are potential forms of consciousness entirely different. We can go through life without suspecting their existence.

-William James

Fear is an active participant for many upon meeting the visitors, a fear similar to the fear of death. Many contactees report that they realize that their fear was subjective and stemmed primarily from contact with the unknown.

One of the steps in my quest to understand the reactions of others and mine in addressing the unknown, began when I found parallels between the experience of clinical death (near-death experience/NDE) and the experience of meeting the visitors.

Studying the relationship between them may help us understand the stories of people who have experienced negative abductions, and those who have felt transcendence and pleasant experiences. Also, we may understand a little more about the contact with the entities many people report during clinical death.

The special nature of that experience was first communicated to me by my family. It turned out that my grandmother, my mother, and two sisters had all gone through clinical death[1] where they left the body, making me wonder if this could run in families?(*My grandmother continued to live for many more years after the incident, and my sisters are still alive and well today.)*

---

[1] Clinical death is a temporary condition where the heart stops beating and supplying blood and oxygen to the brain, yet brain tissue cells are still alive, but no brainwave activity is recorded in the measuring instruments. In some cases, which are not sufficiently understood, after a while, the dead person comes back to life, his heart begins to beat, and he returns to breathing. Thus, the previous state of death is redefined as "temporary death" - clinical.

In many cases, the NDErs describe what they experienced while they were defined as dead, as a clear feeling of being self-conscious and very self-aware in the journey between the world of life and another world.

Many doctors claim that this strange experience of returning to life, is nothing but the result of some brain activity that creates hallucinations... or is it?

To better understand what is going on in these moments, here is an example of my grandmother's experience.

My grandmother was about 45 at the time and lived in Isfahan, Iran. She unknowingly suffered from a weakness in her heart, and one day she had a severe heart attack. Her son, who was close to her at that moment, rushed into town and ordered a doctor. When the same doctor examined her and found her condition, he gave her a shot with a medication he thought would help her, but shortly after she received the injection, her condition worsened, and she stopped breathing. There was nothing left for the doctor to do but to determine the time of her death.

The word that she had died got around very quickly, and many neighbors, close relatives, and acquaintances, flocked to her house to converge around her body. As they gathered and began mourning, the doctor covered her body with a sheet and went about his business.

Some time went by, and my uncle, my grandmother's son, was not only mournful but also feeling guilty for calling in the doctor at whose hands she died. He blamed himself and was beyond consoling. At some point, he removed the sheet from her face, laid her head on his knees, and wept.

My uncle told my mother that while he was crying, he looked into his mother's face. His tears fell on her cheeks, and he saw her lips begin to move. He asked for a glass of water with sugar and dripped it into her mouth.

She woke up.

After a few days, she told my mother that she clearly remembered the moment she died and left her own body. From her view from above, she saw the room with her body on the bed and she continued floating up through the roof of the house. She could see around the entire neighborhood; she saw the people coming to the courtyard, she heard what they said, and she felt their feelings.

She said she felt wonderful and that she was aware of what was going on, including the sight of her son crying on her covered body.

She continued her ascent and arrived in the 'afterlife' or the 'other world,' where she was asked whether she would like to go back to her body. Driven by her sheer will to take away the pain her son felt, she strove to come back to her own body, back to life.

When my grandmother recounted this experience, it was clear to her she had indeed left her own body and returned to it. She was able to report what was going on all around her during the time she was out of her own body until she occupied it again.

There is no rational explanation that could account for the fact that my grandmother was able to see down to her physical, corporeal body, dozens of feet out of the bed she was resting on, with her grieving family gathered around her. Likewise, there is no physical way to hear and see several things or places at once, but she did; she saw the people coming out of their homes, and at the same time, she saw her immediate family inside.

However hard to fathom, the answer is quite simple; my grandmother's consciousness experienced everything that was going on without her body's mediation.

Most of the people who recall their near-death experience, leaving their body and returning to it, describe it in an amazingly similar way; they recount how their consciousness continued to be aware of its surroundings, how they were completely free of the body's pains and limitations, how they felt this existential bliss the like of which they never experienced before, and could not account for. Many of them also recalled wonderful music.

Countless people in many different places and cultures around the world describe the same situation when they see their bodies lying motionless, and also see the doctors or family members who are near the body.

They describe how they can see, hear, and even feel the world they have just separated from! Some may even provide information about people who were out of the room at that time!

Most of the people who experienced an NDE describe a tunnel they passed through on their way from our known world to some other place, the hereafter, or another world at the other end of the tunnel, from where pleasant, incredibly beautiful light was emanating, guiding them towards it.

There, on the other side of the tunnel, at the mount of "the afterlife," as various religions refer to it, or, in Judaism, "the word of truth," AKA "the next world," those people are greeted by spirits, angels or relatives who have already passed on. They have come to greet the newcomers, help them, guiding them in the transition to the new place.

Up to a point before crossing over to the other side of the tunnel, the accounts are very similar. Nevertheless, the identity of the beings who came to help them on the other side of the tunnel is different; each person recounts a unique and different story about the identity of the beings.

Some people describe their entry into the "other side" as consisting of a welcoming party of their loved ones who had died before they did, people whom they loved and cherished in particular, like a grandparent, a spouse, a loved one, a relative or a friend. Other accounts include spiritual figures who came to greet them.

Others, like my mother, describe the patriarchs, Abraham, Isaac, and Jacob. Some are greeted by the prophet Elijah, some met Jesus or angels. Others saw the Buddha.

All say they were greeted lovingly. Often, they were asked whether they would like to relinquish their corporeal body once and for all and move on, or whether they would like to return to their body.

It turns out that most of the people who had this experience felt the same immense love, be it from people who were close to them in life, or spiritual figures who emanated their unconditional love.

In most cases, the figures they encountered were in line with their belief system. Jews were greeted by rabbinical or biblical figures, Christians by Jesus or one of his apostles, and so on.

These correlations between one's beliefs and the beings on the other side of the tunnel have given rise to the claim that the whole 'out-of-body experience' and 'clinical death' are but the product of that person's own subjective tastes, affiliations, and perceptions in life, or worldview. They conclude that the whole story is merely the figment of one's imagination contrived by the hallucinating mind.

But does this skeptical view of "explaining everything away" make any sense?

Could it be a mere "coincidence" that so many people of different eras, cultures, and locations experience the same "hallucination" of leaving their body and looking into a room from the outside? They talk about the same tunnel, the same light, the same greeting by loving, caring beings.

Could it not be that at some point, something is taking place of which we do not have sufficient understanding?

From my point of view today, this appears to be the case.

Those same spiritual beings who greet people on the other side of the tunnel are free from the definitions of the world we know. Like anything else that is connected with the spiritual plane, they are set very much apart from our known world. They are very different from our own reality. They do not have a set, pre-determined shape, or any fixed-configuration, complete with a definite time and place. Such fixed things are part and parcel of our world, for they are but the only forms of expression with which we can communicate and understand.

The experience of the beings from this other place or spiritual world lingers only as a memory once those people return to their bodies. Then the body is a functioning system again, complete with a heart that pumps blood and oxygen to a fully conscious brain.

That brain is translating what the unconscious mind had experienced, and it is doing that by forming it into something familiar and logical, something which is recognizable to the known physical world. We do this subconsciously when we attempt to define our abstract recollection in terms of familiar characters, whom we deem similar or close enough to that abstract experience.

Our mind views the surrounding world by learning to associate and extrapolate only from the known and familiar reality.

This follows us around and builds up from the moment we are born, so when someone has a near-death experience, the lingering memory of the whole experience is indeed still tied to the physical reality which he knows.

After people cross through the tunnel and get further away from their corporeal body and the terms of the physical world, things do change. The hereafter, or the afterlife, does indeed follow a different set of rules. Our perception of time and place fades. Instead, a new consciousness unfolds, free of the constraints we have known from our everyday lives, forcing a shape and a tangible configuration onto anything and everything. The dimension we refer to as the afterlife comprises loving beings.

After the return to the material body, it is difficult to grasp and recall those loving beings from our abstract memory, so we attach them to our known world and describe them to ourselves in those terms. We cannot define something that has but a formless essence. That which is not dual in nature – we can only experience, but not fully comprehend by our normal, dual, rational thinking.

Therefore, the way these entities are defined varies from person to person. To one person, the same sense of love and confidence he experiences from that being, now translated and defined into a certain character, perhaps as a loving relative he knew in his life; for another person, it is a loving, spiritual figure in whom he has believed all his life.

In conclusion:

It is hard for us to logically accept such a different reality, to grasp a reality where our familiar definitions and boundaries do not exist.

However, the very fact that at least some of us remember the experience on the other side of the tunnel indicates that we have the ability to experience and tap into that dimension.

Just because each of us remembers and translates an indefinite entity in a particular and different way from one another, does not negate the very essence of that being as he saw it.

This is something we can understand only by experiencing it.

In the space beyond the other side of the tunnel, all the various possibilities exist together as ONE.

People who have encounters with visitors encounter the same phenomenon as the tunnel experience. In this instance too, the ET's appearance, as part of the meeting with a human being, cannot escape being translated by the person who meets them into the form his or her mind assigns. This is the way the mind grasps, processes, and stores the information.

When it comes to my one encounter with the visitors, they looked like this:

Nevertheless, they did help me realize that the image I gave them, their actual appearance to me, is also related to me personally, to the way I perceive.

On another occasion when I made contact, I asked them for an explanation of their appearance.

I received the answer through automatic writing:

We know your way of seeing us. But you can't
see us the same way you see your world. You're

still trying to see us through your normal vision possibility of the physical dimension. Now you see our unclear flashes, these are the flashes of starting a new vision, and that is still incomprehensible to you.

We look to you now in the way you choose and able to see.

The way you see us is defined by you. We look the way you see us as a result of sharing your perception of our existence, but we have no definite form.

Over time, you will be able to understand that an invisible essence for you can also be defined in terms of your perception. That essence can show to you definite, only when your physical perception participates in some form of that essence and binds it with your own choice.

When we visit your world, we are also temporarily defined in a certain physical body, but that is not the only form or our original essence. In our dimension, there is no need for a physical body defined in a certain way as you do. A body with such boundaries guarantees the legality of existence and consciousness in the reality of your world.

You participate in the definitions of reality that you are given, but you are not yet aware of it.

In the next chapter, I present how modern science also seems to reveal the same dilemma in interpreting reality. The behavior of the subatomic particles reveals a distinct reality in which the laws of nature are completely different. It is the same process by which our consciousness intervenes and translates our reality.

Here is a related quote from David Bohm, who has been described as one of the most significant theoretical physicists of the 20th century and who contributed unorthodox ideas to quantum theory, neuropsychology, and the philosophy of mind.

The quote is about the nature of the quantum particles that are the invisible basis of the substance on our world:

Both faces always hide in the texture of the quantum, but the way the viewer meets the texture determines which face will appear and which will remain hidden.

--David Bohm

"Wholeness and the Implicate Order"

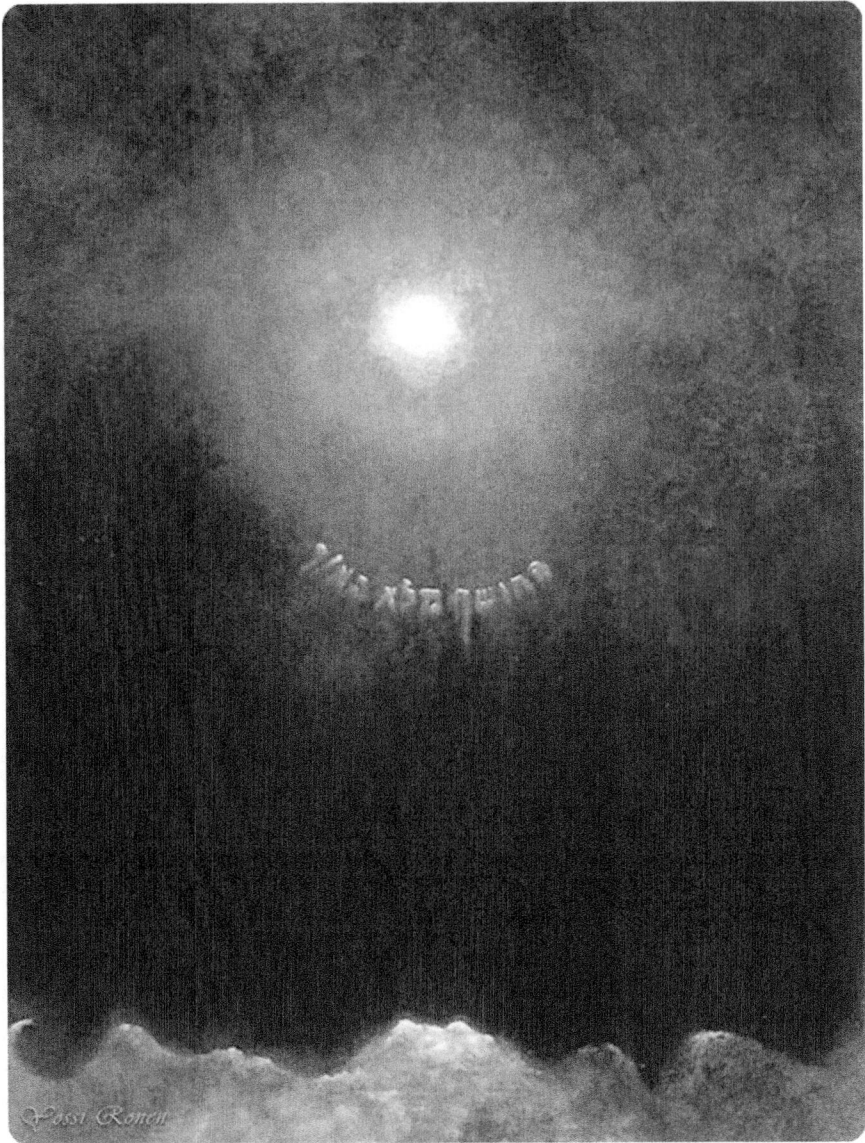

Figure 1 The darkness is full of light.

Seven

Quantum Mechanics and the Visitors

Everything in reality that we call real, is made up of things we cannot say are real.

--Nils Bohr

Nobel Prize in Physics (1922)

The same strange and unexpected truth that is revealed in the study of the subatomic field is also present in the encounter with the visitors and also at the time of clinical death. They all have a common denominator; the borders of time and space break down.

Quantum mechanics was born in the early 20th century following experiments with the study of the behavior of atoms and the smallest particles of matter, such as electrons and photons.

Even if the general public and the physicists themselves do not quite understand the logical possibility of quantum theory, it is considered as being the most accurate and successful in all of scientific history and the most important intellectual achievement of the 20th century.

According to quantum physics, the smallest particles of matter can exist and be measured in two completely different forms, both as a wave or as a particle.

The subatomic units of matter are very abstract two-faced entities. They sometimes appear as particles (like balls) and sometimes as waves - depending on how they are viewed. And this dual nature is also revealed by the light (photons), which can take the form of electromagnetic waves or particles.
--Fritjof Capra
The Tao of Physics

The significance of this fact is revolutionary in terms of understanding our material world. Particles that are the basis of the physical world we know, actually exist in two completely different forms at the same time. But when we observe them, we can only see one of their modes of existence, as a wave propagating in space, or as a solid particle at a certain point.

The principle of uncertainty that Warner Heisenberg (winner of the Nobel Prize for Physics) defines, says that the electron in its wavy state is not in a definite place; it is "here" and "there" together, like a cloud that can only be statistically known.

The electron particle in its wavy state was given the name - "superposition."

After its measurement, when the electron appears as a particle defined in time and place - its state is called - "position."

The "position" is the particular pattern and definition that the electron received through our measurement.

Today, some scientists say that it is possible to see and prove in laboratory experiments that these small particles respond to our consciousness, the behavior of the particle in the experiment varies depending on the observer.

Here is an explanation from a quantum mechanics physicist:

Everything, in reality, we call real is made of things
we can't say are real
-Nils Bohr

It is difficult for us to digest this sentence because it does not make sense, but perhaps the way to understand it is to accept that there is a layer in our reality that is not real nor made for our ordinary perception.

My hypothesis is that quantum reality is, in fact, a glimpse of another dimension. Possibly the ability of today's scientific world to prove the existence of that quantum world is only the discovery of the tip of the iceberg of the vast space in that dimension.

The new revelations showing that these particles respond to the observer's consciousness, give us a hint that there is a connection between our consciousness and that dimension of subatomic particles. So, in a way, it is the same dimension.

We can see the connection between the two different modes of these particles, a wave, or a particle - and the experience of our consciousness in its two basic modes -

the normal state, and its different awareness in clinical death.

When consciousness is not limited to the body and its senses, it experiences the same layer (another dimension) that does not seem real to our everyday knowledge.

During the clinical death experience and on the other side of the tunnel, the time and space experience of our cognition are different; they are boundless and not defined, a situation similar to "superposition."

After awakening from the experience, the perception of reality returns to its usual place, and we are forced to translate and materialize the memory of the experience. This defines and limits it to a form, to a particular thing in time and place. This perception is similar to the situation of "position."

After the "measurement" by our ordinary consciousness, the experience of all possibilities beyond the tunnel is forced to collapse into one familiar definite option.

Only now it can be given a familiar name.

The abstract, formless, and immense love received on the other side of the tunnel, when one has regained normal consciousness, now needs a clear definition of the source of this love that he experienced there. What was it? Jesus? An angel? My beloved grandfather?

This is the result of our natural perception of reality, a form of perception that makes it difficult for us to see all the possibilities of different expressions in one space.

Our dualistic point of view means that we can only see a particle or a wave, but not both together.

It seems like that for us, viewing the wave collapses its function and we then view it only as a particle.

We separate when we notice there is a difference.

"Quantum theory thus reveals a basic oneness of the universe. It shows that we cannot decompose the world into independently existing smallest units. As we penetrate into matter, nature does not show us any isolated "building blocks," but rather appears as a complicated web of relations between the various parts of the whole. These relations always include the observer in an essential way. The human observer constitutes the final link in the chain of observational processes, and the properties of any atomic object can be understood only in terms of the object's interaction with the observer."
--Dr. Fritjof Capra - "The Tao of Physics"

Light and matter are both single entities, and the apparent duality arises in the limitations of our language.

"There is a fundamental error in separating the parts from the whole, the mistake of atomizing what should not be atomized. Unity and complementarity constitute reality."
--Werner Heisenberg

Automatic writing:

Your reality is exactly what our reality is. There is only one reality.

The difference in perception and experience of reality between us is only in the translation of that reality.

Reality itself is not up to you or us, and it already exists and is a given.

The same reality that already exists and is not implied by two faces or more is actually the only reality—the Divine in your language.

The same reality that is not up to you - the Divine Reality, is one reality that also includes your interpretations of it!

The one truth is still incomprehensible to your understanding. It is not defined in any way; it is beyond the good or bad separation according to your dual standards - it contains an expression of communication and connection. In your language, you can say - love.

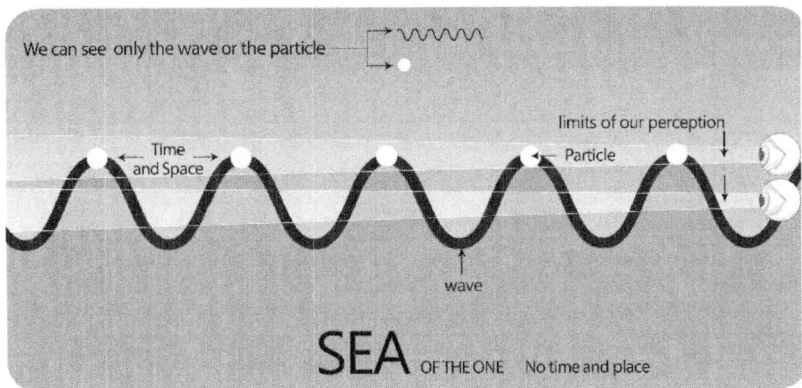

This is a diagram of the way I see the unity of the wave and the particle as it is revealed to us as separate from each other by our scientific tools. The sea signifies the complete space, the unified field of both. In the laboratory, we can only measure its wavy expression or only its expression as a particle that is in a given time and place. In fact, these are different expressions of the same thing - the waves and their rounded edges are of the same one sea. The wave/ particle paradox is created in our perception. We see the distinctions of the different expressions in the ONE – as separate.

Eight

A Dream State Study Preparing for Contact

Sometime after my unsuccessful attempt to meet them face to face again, the visitors created a meeting between us.

It was created through a long-detailed dream in the early morning.

(At the end of this chapter, I write how I received the physical sign that it was not an ordinary dream, but an actual meeting that was held through a dream.)

The purpose of the dream that they created was about the experience and the main challenge for us to establish communication with the visitors, this is something they are as interested in as we are.

Here is an accurate description of the dream itself. What follows is my understanding of the message and the meaning of it.

The dream began at its end, at its final purpose, the contact.

The dream began with a feeling of excitement, knowing that the guests were now close. A meeting between us was about to happen.

I am with hundreds of other people near the beach in Jaffa, Israel. There are green, grassy hills and it is morning, clean and fresh air blows in from the sea, the sun is radiating a soft, full light, above and around the sky that is a smooth and bright blue.

Some people stand and talk to each other casually; others sit or lie calmly on their backs as they face the sky with their eyes closed.

A group of individuals moves slowly among the people who are lying on their backs, they are kneeling when they begin to heal and treat us. Slowly, with patience and love, they move their hands over the body and gently touch the people's chests and foreheads. They were going from one to another.

To my delight they come to me too, I lie on my back, one of them looks into my eyes, smiles, and slowly moves his palms over my torso. I immediately feel the heat from his hands pass to me too, his hands warming my body and re-thawing my heart - streaming my feelings. Until then, I wasn't even aware that my body was cold. Now my emotions are flowing, in my body like warm water, and I feel comfortable, my body relaxes and finally rests. His glittering eyes are staring into mine the entire time; he has only pure love for me/us. He tells me something ...

I have explicit knowledge of mass healing, spreading in every direction, working beyond place, and time.

The dream goes on; in a split second, I am suddenly elsewhere and find myself in an empty movie theater.

Sitting in one of the soft, red armchairs in the middle of the hall, I look at the large screen across from me with a smile of familiarity. By the screen, the visitor standing looking directly at me, and I realize that I am within a dream.

I know it's a dream through which the guest tries to talk to me about something I will find useful after I wake up.

He speaks to me through his eyes; I understand his words, and it pleases me to hear what he says to me, but I also realize that I probably won't remember anything he says now, after waking up from the dream.

The visitor also understands this. He consults with others I cannot see, and I know that the dream is about to change.

My body begins to rise from the chair without my intention, floating in the air and slowly approaching the screen. As my body advances towards the screen, I am getting smaller and smaller and younger and younger until I am a very small baby. I move so close to the screen that I can now see the space between the lines of the screen's wire structure.

My body, which has now become so tiny that it can move into the screen and penetrate the spaces between the thin crisscrossed wires that make up the screen.

On the other side of the screen, I find myself in a moist, dark tunnel, where dim light is beginning to show at the other end, and it leads me inside towards him.

As I move through the tunnel to where light is approaching, I lose the memory of the things I was told before I enter the tunnel. The notion that I'm dreaming now, is forgotten.

I didn't know where the tunnel was leading to. I found myself floating forward towards the light at the end of the tunnel. My body grows now, like a 6-year-old boy.

I stepped out from the tunnel and into a dark place. As I walked among trees, fear began to creep up on me, not remembering the tunnel, how I got there, or why I was there. Up in the trees, I saw black forms of objects that I didn't recognize; I approached them carefully. It's a children's courtyard. I was in kindergarten and it was night time! There were swings, a skating rink, a carousel...

From the top of one of the children's slides among the trees, I saw a hand that was waving and it motioned for me to approach. I noticed it was the familiar figure of a childhood friend. He invited me to join him upstairs. Climbing the ladder of the slide, I settled in comfortably next to him. Glad to be with him, I was no longer alone in the dark woods.

We both admired the view around us and above the treetops. Suddenly he raised his hand, pointing his finger at a point of light over the horizon.

I looked in the direction he pointed to. Above the horizon, a lighted object approached us. At first, I thought it was a plane with its headlights illuminating our area, but as it got closer, I found I was wrong. It had a large, long, cylindrical body, which looked almost black. It was a huge, long, air cylinder, with light emanating from it inside of it which was coming out from its windows.

As this "air train" approached us, I was delighted and excited by what I saw through those transparent windows; each window was lit by a yellow-orange light, a robust but soft and pleasant light.

Out of the windows, the visitors' faces gazed, some sitting at the window, and some walking along the cylinder train. I felt so much joy seeing them, I quickly waved hello, but at that moment, my friend panicked and reached up to lowered my hand... I realized I was doing something wrong! I made the mistake of waving my hand. Now they know exactly where I am ... and.... they'll probably catch me.

Seized with anxiety, deep fear began to grow and take control of me; all I wanted now was to get away, to escape from that place, and as quickly as possible.

Frightened, I got off the slide and started running back through the trees, away from where they saw me. As I ran, I heard someone chasing me, and even more panic and the fear of death overtook me. I was running to save my life!

The pursuers were catching up to me and would get me any moment. I finally reached the high fence that surrounded the garden, climbed it quickly, and leaped to the other side.

As soon as my feet touched the ground, almost breathless from the horror and running, I looked back to see the pursuers. I was amazed at what I saw - on the high fence trying to climb after me was a little girl visitor; with one hand she held an ice cream, it was melting and running between her long fingers, down her hand and almost to the elbow. Her big, black eyes sparkled with tears. She laughed and cried at the same time because I ran away from her. She wanted to play with me!

I realized I was the one scaring myself.

Now my body appeared a little older, a young boy. My attention shifted to the large building next to me, across the fence. The building aroused my curiosity; it was a school.

I went towards the building, and after finding its main door, I entered it; it was indeed a deserted school. There was not a living soul inside. The school was mostly dark, but there was a faint light coming from one of the doorways at the end of the corridor I was walking down. Carefully, I approach the lighted doorway and entered; it was a big, desolate, sports hall.

Entering the silent hall, I heard the echo of my footsteps on the wooden floor. There were dark doorways along the round hall. As I examined the ladders and training equipment in the room, I heard the sound of barefoot steps approaching. The sound of additional approaching steps was also heard coming from all the entrances to the hall.

Walking away from the doorways to the center of the hall, I stood scared, waiting to see who would come into the hall. As soon as it happened, I felt a shock as if a current of electricity passed through me and a chill shook my body.

Through each of the dark openings, unidentified, thin figures entered the hall, their bodies wrapped in robes similar to monks' robes that were inlaid with black and green; large hooded cloaks covered most of their faces and reached down to the floor.

Slowly, and from all directions, they approached me with measured steps, their faces are hidden.

I didn't know who they were or what they wanted from me; they came close to me but didn't show their faces or say anything. As they approached about six feet away from me, I saw their long fingers and realized these were the visitors I was trying to escape.

Now, I was even more frightened, knowing, and already aware of their immense power and ability to know my thoughts and the depths of my soul. They came close and started slowly walking around me in a circle; I knew they were staring at me, their eyes measuring me from under their hoods.

I stood in the middle of the circle, helpless, as the fear in me grew; they moved around me carefully, examining me and penetrating every cell in my body, bearing in mind who they were going to tussle with. Terrified, I watched them as I knew there was no chance of winning or escaping them.

One of them suddenly lunged towards me and reached his long hand to touch my body; I defended myself and pushed his hand away. Another one approached me and tried to touch me, and I struggled with him too.

In one quick moment, as if in a coordinated decision, everyone converged towards me, and with their movements getting faster, they tried to strike me with their hands.

The visitors walked around me faster as each one of them tried to hit me, and I evaded them by defending myself. The speed of their movements increased until I could no longer keep up with them. No one had touched me yet, but it seemed the battle was lost.

From time to time I glimpsed the black and large eyes of the guests who constantly lowered their heads under the hood, and saw clear flashes of threat and a desire to kill me, the swing of their hands still striving to hit me. They also began trying to kick me with their feet.

No longer could I defend myself. The crumpled green hand of one of them connected as he beat my torso. I was utterly shocked by his contact with my body, out of fear and disgust, I ducked and bent down to throw up.

As soon as I bent and my head was lower than the height of the stranger's head attacking me, I was able to take a look at him and see his face under the headgear ...

He was smiling.

Stunned, I quickly looked away to the other visitors around me. They were smiling too, smiling at me.

I lowered my arms to protect my body, and as if in slow motion, I saw the other guests' hands coming closer and closer, touching my waist and ... trying to tickle me.

The circle of guests around me kept moving. As soon as they saw and felt that I was not afraid of them anymore, that I realized they were not trying to hurt me, just tickle, they raised their heads and showed me their smiling faces. We started laughing. As my fear faded, in its place came the joy, joy that flows from us, from one to the other. The wall of fear inside me disappeared, and a burst of pleasure and deep blissful, pure happiness filled me.

In those moments, I realized that I was able to remove the barriers inside of me. Now, those are memories of connecting and healing between us all in the circle, between the worlds, my world, and their world. I felt the fear release me. Knowing the soothing truth filled me with confidence, physical strength, and peaceful power.

We kept going around in a circle, now and then we tickled each other, each of us laughing with each other and that feeling grew even more. The feeling of liberation and joy grew and vibrations of happiness filled our bodies until we started to dance in the circle with one another and occasionally we jumped around like kids. Our movements became a collective dance, we danced and jumped with our feet and our hands as the laughter grew ...

The dance incident had become an experience of ever-increasing happiness, in or out of which joyous and intensely rhythmic music emerged.

I felt like a bouncy, happy child filled with circular energy that was growing and growing around us. The feeling of joy created a mental transcendence, an experience that extended my consciousness even further. I had experienced everyone in a circle with me and around me, felt them inside of me, and we had a common language, a primary language, without words that allowed for boundless understanding.

New insight washed over me, every sliver of the feeling of horror I had felt before, now becoming another part of the feeling of happiness.

I experienced the simple and basic essence of me, of my soul.

Waking from the dream, I couldn't remember it right away but still smiled. I was awake and staring at the window; by dawn, I realized I woke up very early but felt so vigorous that I got out of bed carefully not to wake my sleeping companion by my side. Her beautiful eyes were closed, her face calm and a hint of a smile on her lips.

Going to the kitchen, walking in my body felt different, full of rare energy. I also felt so optimistic and happy that I began to walk around the room to relax into that fantastic and strange feeling. What was happening to me? Dimly I remembered that I had a long and full dream, and woke up with a childish smile.

Through that smile, I tried to step back and remember the dream and began to faintly recall the music I heard at the end of it, and then I stopped breathing for a moment, as the memory of the dream in its entirety flooded me.

If it wasn't an ordinary dream, but a dream that had a real encounter with the visitors, there would be a physical sign. I looked at the back of my hands, and for a second time since the first meeting, I saw, as if through a microscope, the blood flowing through the thin capillaries in my hands and fingers.

Nine

Decoding from The Dream the Language of Contact with Our Visitors and My Translation

During the time from the first meeting to today, the visitors have come up with several dreams designed to help me understand and cope with the contact. They differ completely from ordinary dreams, being clear and detailed, not like my subjective dreams. For many years now, I continue to explore the depths of these dreams.

In the dream from the previous chapter that the visitors "created" for me, part of the sequence of events in the dream did not flow linearly - that is, from the beginning to the end. The dream began with the experience of the practical results I gained from experiencing it. It begins with the experience of the purpose of the sequence of events that will take place in it afterward.

It started from its conclusion ending – a healing process for us that involved an encounter with them.

Learning the process of the healing itself started afterward, in the cinema. I sat there as if in a lesson or a lecture, watching as the visitor explained things to me. He spoke directly to my consciousness.

In the movie theater, I knew that my body was at home and asleep and that I was dreaming of sitting in this lecture hall with the visitor.

After a brief explanation of what seemed like an interesting but complex lecture to me, we both knew that even if I understood it now, I would not remember anything when I woke up.

To solve this dilemma, they decided that the dream experience would change so that their messages would be communicated to me differently, in a more "tangible" way- through the experience of a journey that included events, images, and emotions, more similar to events in the ordinary physical reality I was familiar with.

Here is the translation, in my words, that is close to the way and content of the things I was actually told by this dream. (This is not automatic writing).

The visitors:

Communication from us given to you is other than language.

Our way of thinking is different from yours, but our communication nevertheless exists.

The communication that passes from us to you is fully understood only for the deepest part of your consciousness, a place that is currently almost oblivious to you. It's the place from which your choice of thinking arises. In this primary space of consciousness, you are connected to us and all the life around you. This deep and hidden part of you does understand the information from us since it is also a kind of a language, language of the ONE.

When you become physically aware of your thoughts, it is only after it already takes the shape of words, emotions, or a picture in your mind's/brain's language.

At this point, you are forced to translate and convert the deeper, unconscious Oneness experience into separate, dual concepts, to understand it through separate essences such as a point in time, point in place, distinct shapes and figures, and separate words or names for them. Your mind/brain makes it through finding close associations and memory in your familiar world.

For example, many of you talk about a kind of telepathy in meeting us, since your communication concepts are based solely on broadcast and reception, you also tend to think of the telepathic experience with us as a kind of transmission and reception of one another's thoughts. But in fact, telepathy between us has no transmission or reception. Telepathy operates from a full connection, so at that moment, the information is at the same time on both sides.

Indeed, many of us who have had communication with the visitors say they have received thoughts or even words that have entered their minds in their own language.

Those who find it difficult to accept and incorporate the experience of telepathy, sometimes feel as if the guests are trying to force thoughts into their minds. (I also thought this at the beginning of my encounter.)

The sense of panic and intimidation that we sometimes experience with them seems to be generated by our automatic translation of the experience of the ONE and unity that we do not know and recognize! This experience of unity can scare us; we suddenly experience another consciousness that seems to penetrate our very being. For some, a panic arises and we think, *'What is happening to me'? 'Do I hear voices'?* One can also experience the fear of loss of self-control.

Moreover, the visitors' consciousness is vastly wider than ours in its normal state. The initial experience can cause a feeling of helplessness and you can get lost in that vast space and feels a sense of smallness and a lack of self-confidence, a feeling that you are about to disappear, that you are lost in something much more significant than yourself.

Thus, the experience of Oneness can be translated into a sense of loss of the self, very similar to the fear of death.

Paradoxically, it seems that this purity and innocence of the visitor's consciousness, which allows us to experience Oneness, can sometimes be translated by us as a direct threat and even perceived as a violent experience.

At the height of the dream the visitors created for me in the school gymnasium, I stopped being afraid only when they showed their faces, and I saw that they were actually smiling. It was their way of showing me how my rational fear blocked me from perceiving the whole picture. This fear separates us from the love that is there, and from our deeper self, our soul, and the vast spaces to which it is connected.

The visitors are aware of this fear that exists within us; they know that contact with the boundaries of our conscious mind with the unknown is currently the cause of our anxiety. This translated to them that it is not yet the right moment to appear in front of us openly. The direct meeting between humanity and the visitors, and perhaps earlier-the meeting between us and ourselves - will be made possible only when the underlying fear that separates us has disappeared, and on our own initiative.

This may also be one of the reasons why the guests reach out to contact us: they try to help us open up to our consciousness abilities. Our very effort to deal with them, with the fears, to understand who or what they are, leads us to do so!

In our consciousness, there is the potential to connect to the dimension of reality where innocence, unity, and closeness are much more profound. This ability exists in each of us, but currently, most of us are unaware of it and even deny it. For many, innocence is considered a weakness and unrealistic behavior. Growing up, we hardly feel the purity in ourselves; we then mature and harbor no belief in it.

In fact, it is a kind of purity, free from barriers of fear like a glass that allows for transparency and the passage of light through and out of it.

There are countless instances in which this telepathic connection occurs between us, usually in cases where there is emotional closeness, trust, and love, but we treat this with casualness, and not as signs of the natural but fantastic ability that exists in each of us.

I went through a similar situation. It was a wintry night in my new apartment, and I still didn't have any winter blankets. I wrapped up in a thin summer blanket, woke up in the middle of the night, got up and put on a sweater I pulled out of the closet, and went back to sleep.

In the morning, my mom called a little worried and told me she dreamed about me: *"I dreamed you were telling me that you were cold. So, I told you, go to the closet, get a sweater and go back to sleep."*

Ten

Hypnotic Regression

After I spoke about my contact openly, a researcher who had heard about it called me. He offered to regress through hypnosis to reclaim some memories I may have hidden.

He told me that Jacob (a psychiatrist who also deals with the hypnotic regression method) had done many regressions on people who had similar experiences, and he understood this topic.

After overcoming the immediate worry I had in once again experiencing that fear that arose at the beginning of my contact, I agreed.

I was curious to know if there were other events in this encounter that I didn't remember. Another reason that I agreed to the hypnosis was that I decided to write and publish a book about my contact with the visitors, as directly and openly as I could.

I had read about the experience of others who have gone through a similar regression, and I knew that hypnosis could bring additional information from my contact, memories that were pushed deep into my subconscious, possibly because of the natural fear that is sometimes involved in this kind of contact.

I arrived at Jacobs's residence in Holon, frightened, and I stopped in front of his house and lit myself a cigarette. As the fear subsided, I became weak and opaque to the knowledge that there is no reason for any concern, something I already instinctively knew.

I thought that if there were adverse and harsh memories that were uncovered, similar to those I had heard from other encounters, like an abduction, I wanted to find out about them now.

The thought of this caused a stubborn shake in my hand that was already holding another cigarette. I began to seriously think about the possibility of giving up and leaving as long as I could still maintain my sanity. I was worried that this hypnosis might release a hornet's nest of ideas that, for my best interest, should stay dormant ...

In the company of these fears, the aggravated fear, I did not know what to do with myself. On one hand, I wanted to flee from this place, forget the whole thing, but on the other hand, I knew that I could not escape this for my entire life, because this was in me, wherever I might go.

I turned on the light in the stairwell, and with shaking knees, I slowly climbed up to Jacob's apartment.

Jacob opened the door and smiled, through his eyewear, I saw a pair of very delicate and curious eyes, he looked about 50, with a short beard that adorned his face.

The therapist was already waiting in the room. He asked my permission to record the course of hypnosis. I agreed, and he put the tape recorder on the table near me. I briefly told Jacob about the meeting with the visitors and asked him to be prepared for the possibility of me going through the initial shock once again, as I had in my first meeting with them. I asked that the level of hypnosis not go too deep, because to some extent, I wanted to be aware of what was going on around me so I could stay in control. So that I could, if desired, detach myself from the hypnotic regression process.

I also asked Jacob to ensure that I remember every detail of the hypnosis after it was over.

I got his consent. He also tried to calm me down and explained that this is not the first time he has regressed someone who had experienced trauma or had experienced meeting the visitors. With a smile he said, "You have nothing to worry about, I take full responsibility for what I do, and I'm sure that if you would uncover something that you are not aware of, after the regression, you will feel much better - uploading hidden content to the conscious mind, even if it were unpleasant, will help you break free of the feeling of being in jail because of it."

Jacob asked me to sit in the armchair, dimmed the lights, sat in front of me, and asked me to close my eyes and breathe deeply and slowly.

He guided me to relax and feel inner peace. This made me feel much better and I heard his quiet and gentle voice slowly moving away, yet still understood his words.

At his request, I held my right hand in the air above the armrest of the armchair, and Jacob started counting backward. He asked me to alert him when my hand stayed in the air with no effort.

After a few minutes of concentration, I did feel that my body was much lighter, and I could no longer tell if my hand was still in the air or already resting. Jacob instructed me to slowly lay my hands on the armrest. A feeling of pleasant calm and lightness spread throughout my body.

Jacob asked me to come back to the first moment that I clearly remembered when I met face to face with the visitors.

Whispering, I conveyed what I was experiencing.

Jacob briefly repeated my last words "you are in the room sitting on the bed, and several beings are there. One is near you. How do you feel?"

I tell him, "I am extremely confused. Good and bad. I understand and experience tremendous things. I feel I have opened gates into a world that I did not even know existed, but I am also terrified. I am having a hard time. I don't know if I have the strength to hold on. My body is paralyzed... it hurts."

Jacob says, "Let's relax together now. Take a few deep breaths, slowly, yes, you're calmer and quiet. Imagine that you are seeing this all play out like a movie. You are not in pain now. How do you feel?"

Me: "Okay."

Jacob: "Well, now I ask you to look at yourself in that movie... tell me, why do you feel pain? Why is your body paralyzed?"

Me: "From fear ... I don't know ... I'm scared to die ..."

Jacob: "Can you possibly ask them?"

Me: "Yeah, uh, my soul is a bit out of my body, I want to live ..."

Jacob: "Can you let them talk?"

Me/the visitors: "You are afraid because the contact we have built with you, now that you are awake and conscious, face to face with us is difficult for you. It is easier for you to experience us only through the inner consciousness, the part you call your soul, when your body is asleep and unconscious.

The unfamiliar awareness you have between your body and soul, this experience is responsible for much of your body's paralysis.

Since the soul is not physical like your body, it has no lifelike movements in the way that your body recognizes and exists with it. Your body does not understand this experience of total stillness.

When the soul becomes aware (of you) through the body, you feel paralysis, because your body does not know how to contain it, how to live and exist in this stillness.

In terms of the physical body, which exists only within specific boundaries, to be spiritual like a soul which has no boundaries, time, or movement - it instinctively feels like a death warning."

Jacob: "Now, I want to try something with you. Do you feel ok? Are you ready to continue, Yossi? Are you with me? You can rest now and concentrate on your place here in the room with us. You're more focused now, more aware of what's going on in the room with me, and what I'm telling you."

Me: "I'm fine, what do you want me to do?"

Jacob: "I want to see if you've already met them before, a meeting you may not remember?"

Me: "Ah ... I don't think such a thing happened. Why you want me to do that?"

Jacob: "It doesn't matter now. We will do a short experiment, and if nothing happens, we will move on."

Me: "Okay, but I feel a little weird; maybe this will prompt me to see something that hasn't happened ..."

Jacob: "No. Together we will easily know if it happened or not."

Me: "Well, I'm ready; what do I do?"

Jacob: "I ask you to imagine a big clock in front of you, the digits will signify years, that is, the numbers mean one year, two years, and so on. This clock is divided into the same number of years as to how old you are now, okay? These numbers in the clock represent your age backward from now: 35, 34, 33, and so on, until you were born, age 0.

Now I want you to see the clock dials moving backward from now; it is moving back in time. I ask you to pay attention if the dial stops on a specific year, and if it does, tell me what year it is, okay?"

Me: "I understand your request, but I still feel like you're asking me to invent something through my imagination ..."

Jacob: "It's okay, don't worry, I know what we're doing, and you can count on me, and yourself too, to observe if it did or didn't happened, ok?

Take a few deep breaths, slowly, calm down and come back inside ... imagine the watch ... you see the clock dial now? Start moving it back."

I looked at that clock I created in my mind, and as Jacob asked me, I imagined the handset moving back year after year ...

(I was thinking: "...This is all in my imagination, I determine what happens there, it's my watch ...")

The time kept moving back in my mind ...

I gave up those thoughts and allowed the watch and the dial to continue without "interfering" with me as if I was watching a movie ...

The handset suddenly stopped in front of the number 3.

"Age 3," I said, smiling in disbelief.

Jacob: "All right, now I want you to take a few deep breaths and feel comfortable and relaxed. You are now 3 years old, where are you?"

Me: "I'm in my (childhood) hometown - Rishon Le Zion, I'm playing in the orange grove next to my house."

Jacob: "Do you see anything else?"

Me: "Ah ... I'm playing with dry leaves; they have a nice noise and a pleasant smell when I play with them. There are all kinds of things going on around here, I see ants... The air is balmy, I like to come here, alone. I love playing with dry branches ... Ah, I hear a familiar sound from above, something which is black and small like a bird approaching from afar, it is not a bird, oh it comes to me, stands on the ground near the trees, has a round shape with a rounded dome, made of black material, like a hard and robust sponge, I run up to it, I'm thrilled and happy, he opens the door and invites me to come in ... "

Me: I started laughing ... "You don't see what's going on? I'm now inventing a spaceship that has come to take me ..."

Jacob: "Just continue on. Don't worry, go back inside, you're calm now, and no matter if ... you are just watching a movie now, ok? Keep telling me what you see ... "

Me: "He invites me to come in."

Jacob: "Who invites you in?"

Me: "It's the same little creature with the big black eyes that was standing next to me in my room."

Jacob: "How do you feel with him? What do you see? What are you doing now?"

Me: "He shows me his spacecraft, it's small, and he is the only one in it, it has one more chair, maybe a screen or it is a big window, there are all kinds of things here which I don't understand. We're good friends, we know each other, very happy to see and be with each other... I am excited and want to play with him, he tells me that we are now on a trip, he wants to show me something."

Jacob: "Tell me ... what do you see?"

Me: "We got up, I see the orchard disappearing through the big windows, we are going somewhere... it's black all-around, and I see stars, it's beautiful. He is explaining to me all kinds of things, new things, and I understand him ... understand him very well. I enjoy hearing it, but I can't remember what he tells me ...

... We have reached his world.

The spacecraft's door opens quietly, there is only silence outside, a bright orange-and-pink light comes in through the door, we head out... down to the ground. We are on a beach with rocky but clean sand. The sea is huge, just huge.

The water is a pink-orange turquoise, above the sea is a turquoise sky and two large circles, distant balls, maybe suns or moons ... radiating a delicate, faint light, they have a bright orange and white color that casts its light down to the water and sand.

He and I are now walking on the beach..."

At that moment in hypnosis, a strong and misunderstood excitement began to hold me ...

"We walk together slowly. We feel comfortable together; we talk all the time; he tells me all kinds of things ... We are close to each other; we hold hands.

I look at the beach; it is blue and pink, gray-colored. There are crystalline rocks all around. There are buildings on other big rocks, groups of structures built on the crest of the rocks, and each of them has a vast transparent dome, the dome is around and above the houses."

I returned to being aware of myself sitting in Jacob's chair. For some reason, the feeling of excitement grew more and more, my closed eyes were blinking almost madly. Tears flowed from my eyes.

I did not understand what was happening to me; I felt very excited, but I did not understand why. Why are tears running from my eyes? Am I crying? Or are my eyes just searing because of the strange blinking motion that is now gripping my eyes? I couldn't stop the blinking. I couldn't control it.

Jacob: "Do you feel good? Do you want to rest?"

It's hard for me to answer him. I think that if I try to speak now, a weird whine will burst outside me.

Jacob: "Yossi, take a few deep breaths, are you ok? Please tell me what you feel."

Me: "I ... I know this place."

At that moment, in a split second, a massive eruption of memories floods me. It was the communication that took place there between the visitor and me.

In an instant, I was filled with so many memories, I could fill a small book.

But I couldn't open my mouth or say anything yet to Jacob.

Allow me to clarify:

Writing this part was among the most challenging and complex parts of the book. Even today, I can say that I do not fully understand it.

Nevertheless, I had to translate the communication that occurred when it was without words, and when my mentality was that of a kid.

I am trying here to convey the communication, voices, and feelings of that kid I remembered, as much as I can, without the interference of my adult mentality, which is now writing about the experience.

Here is the translation of this memory:

There was silence. There was no sign of plants or birds around; everything was clean, too clean, there was no breeze, no sign of clouds. He and I were walking on the shoreline, he talks to me in his way, without saying a word aloud, but we understand each other. He knows what I think about what he tells me. And so do I – I know his every thought and feeling.

I look down, watching the ground, the large grains of sand that glitter like glass from time to time. The light is weak and soft but loaded with something, similar to our sunsets.

I feel good; my body is small. When we look at each other in the eyes, it's straight and close – we are of the same height.

He and I are holding hands; he is small but also not; he remembers all, knows so much, and is very intelligent; his skin is green and slightly wrinkled, like that of an ancient man.

Many times, I laugh, and so does he, but his mouth doesn't move at all. Only his eyes have smiles, a glitter of joy.

I look at the domes that surround the houses ...

Me: "Why...?"

Him: "One can't live here otherwise ... the air has changed. We've ruined it. We now live in bubbles we had to build for ourselves."

Me: "What happened?"

Him: "We started to forget."

Me: "Forget what?"

Him: "The connection to ourselves, that is, the connection between things - God."

Me: "I Don't understand, what happened?"

Him: "First, we started to lose the connection to ourselves. Then between each other, and then to the relationship with all the things around us. The closest interpretation of this relationship to everything, in your language, is – to God, or, to One."

Me: "So, God was angry and punished you?"

It seems that the question tickled him, and he laughed without moving his mouth, and that made me laugh.

Him: "One is the connection; this is the connection and acceptance between things. Anger is the opposite ..."

Me: "Uh ... I see ... so, what happened here? How come you, the animals, and the plants now only live in closed bubbles?"

Him: "... we created a distance, unknowingly, between ourselves, and then between the world around us. In your world this is also starting now. We caused something like what you call an "ecological holocaust," a holocaust that began within us – by ignoring our connection within our psyche, we then began to ignore the link that unites between all things, what you call God. Because that one God is in us all, ignoring him within ourselves, is ignoring him everywhere else."

Me: "You speak in riddles, I'm not sure I understand ... what does this have to do with me, with my world?"

Him: "That is what this is all about. The context of things."

This concept of "God" is incomprehensible to me.

Me: "Can you explain to me without the concept of 'God'? It confuses me."

Him: "Yes, I'm talking about the connection to yourself or to other things in general, do you understand this?"

Me: "Yes."

Him: "Well, it started when our heart's attention departed from the feeling we have between things. And this connection is also to the One, to everything.

So, the distance continued on to the relationship between us and our world. The same thing is happening now in your world.

At the very basis of the existence of the universe, there is a connection between you and me, between my world and yours.

You are here, in my 'world' because what has happened here is very much related to what is happening in your world, and it also works in the opposite direction - it is mutual.

It all happens because that which connects between things is the same."

Me: "Explain this to me ... what does this connection between the worlds look like? What does it sound like?"

Him: "It is like one thread that holds and connects things ..."

He knew I didn't understand this well ...

Him: "Well, I'll try to show you ... Let's collect some small stones."

We collected some small stones from the ground.

He held several stones in his palm and looked deep into my eyes and said: "You see, every stone represents a specific thing - a world."

Me: "Yes."

He pulled a long string from my shirt, and with the string in his hand, he touched the stones, each of them formed a hole in the middle of it."

Me: "How do you do that?"

Him: "It is not a problem; you can do it too. I'll show you later."

He threaded the string inside the stones and tied both ends.

Him: "Here, you see? One thread that holds things together, it connects the worlds."

Me: "Is it like a chain of stones, that each stone is a world or a person or a tree for example, and the string is the One?"

Him: "Yes, it is true and beautiful. You might find this a little difficult to understand, but in fact, the stones are also part of the string, and the separate stones are really just one stone, one world.

Our attention in the past has been to our stone (world) and to all other stones that are connected to the string. But today, the focus declined to one stone only, and the thread has been forgotten ... "

Me: "So basically, the thread and all the worlds are one world?"

Him: "One reality, like one world, all is One."

Me: "And what does that one sound like?"

"The same ... if you connect all the sounds, you hear one sound: it's like the air sound that is coming out of your lungs and then throat, before you continue and use it to define something, like a specific sound or word."

Me: "Teach me how to make a hole in the stone with a string from a shirt ..."

Him: "Not a problem, you can do almost anything ... because ... because you are dreaming now."

Me: "What? Dreaming? So, everything that's going on right now, this world, and you, it's all just a dream I'm having? It is my imagination that I'm making up and I'm not really here at all?"

He started laughing again; this time, he leaps about, laughing.

Him: "Sure, you're here, don't you see ...?" He said, continuing to laugh. I felt embarrassed.

Him: "Didn't you ask yourself how it is that the air here is contaminated, and yet you're still breathing without a problem?"

Me: "Uh ...?"

Him: "Don't worry; you're right here. Only your body stays there in the orchard without you (on Earth) it is just like you were falling asleep for a few seconds. "

Me: "Seconds? But we've been here a long time ..."

Him: "Time here is different for you, because without your body, there is no meaning to the time you know. The feeling of time passing from the past through the present to the future is a feeling that belongs to the physical body.

Here, without your body, we can experience in a moment a sequence of things that, in terms of your physical body time, may occur over a lifetime."

Me: "So, what am I doing here? Why is all this happening at all?"

Him: "I've already told you that our worlds are interconnected, interdependent, and therefore responsible for each other. What we do here is related to it. And this is one of our ways of facilitating your (human) communication with us in the future. At this point, you can easily absorb and experience a connection with me because you are not really in your body, you do not depend on your age or your mind, so you can understand what I am saying.

There is a reason why I came to you when you are in your physical body for a short while and have not yet "matured" enough to build the walls between you and your body.

You will wake up soon and go back to your body, you will not be able to accept and understand anything about this encounter.

We have chosen to do it like this so that your consciousness, now within a child's body, can easily store this encounter for many years inside of your body; you will not think about this experience or try to understand it. Then the memory of these moments will remain intact, behind the defensive walls that your himself as he is capable of adult body and mind will create over time.

There is a possibility that in the future when you are older, you will remember this experience and be able to translate it into the words of a mature person and maybe use it."

Me: "Use it?"

Him: "Yes, the memories of this reunion will serve you in the future. In the first phase, the reunion will serve you for yourself. If you choose to speak about it, it will also serve others in your world, and it will serve me and us in my world as well, and eventually also the other dimensions."

Me: "What do you mean?"

Him: "As you grow older in your world, humanity will come to a crucial stage in the evolution of its consciousness into One. We (the visitors) will help and will be part of the same contact with the new realms of human consciousness during this time, even if most of humanity would not yet be ready to know or accept this information concisely.

This will be the beginning of humanity's contact with other dimensions in consciousness.

This will be the time when your realization and perception of reality will change in principle, from a mode of knowledge gathering from defined data into a different understanding of reality - through a direct encounter with the reality from which the word derives.

This stage is essential, and it can also be complicated and confusing for you.

The impact of meeting us now will remain with you even in those days; it will enlighten and facilitate the contact and connection between the dimensions in your consciousness and perhaps others.

One of the sensations that those who hear these things, their experience will be that they **know** it, like a familiar but forgotten smell, they will feel that they already **know** and recognize it.

Me: "And how will all this help you? I don't think you're missing anything ..."

Him: "It's very simple; it's still hard for you to understand that we and you...

When we help you, we also help ourselves. When you open up to new dimensions - it's like a new love for you and we're there. So, it's a new love for us too.

When we come to you, we go to ourselves.

In terms of your world - you are the one we are in the past, and when we heal our past, we heal your future – which is our present!"

Me: "What do you mean 'healing'?"

Him: "Healing the ability to contain and experience love.

The essence of the thread that holds the stones, what lies between all things in reality in all its dimensions, is love. And not just the kind of love you know about in human terms. Love is the primary energy of existence and exists in endless ways. It is also an expression of the One. It is the one who sustains everything, and also their connection.

For example, in the human body, there are many organs, and the condition of a disease in a particular organ is essentially a lack of communication and flow into and out of that organ. The disconnection is what blocks the flow of love to and from the environment."

Me: "So, what does this have to do with the things you said before?"

Him: "If we take humanity, for example, the global and personal wars that prevail are the manifestation of the disease that needs healing; you will find it difficult to understand that you (humanity) are one living body and each limb is related to each other.

The individual's personality is not currently connected to himself as he is capable of. Therefore, you create situations in which you suffer and spend much of your life in a lack of love for yourself and so it continues to the environment."

Me: "What happens if we connect with this love you are talking about?"

Him: "You can make a hole in the stone with a sewing thread."

I stopped, watching him in amazement.

Me: "When I asked you how you did that, you said that it wasn't a problem because ... it's just a dream ... and I thought I understood you, now I'm confused again. Maybe <u>you</u> can love everything, but in my reality, it is quite difficult in my world. It is far from the experience of love for everything ... and sometimes only war can bring peace in the end."

Him: "Love is the base of reality because, without it, reality would not be possible at all. Wherever you do not see love, be prepared to accept you not seeing reality as it is."

Me: "So, what is hate anyway? The anger? The evil? Why does it happen?"

Him: "They are 'parts' of the one. It's your human ability to separate things from the whole.

Your thinking separates the bad from the One and chooses not to see the love there. Fear fills it instead. This fear seed grows and gives fruits of pain, anger, hate, and then evil. Sometimes that's how your human freedom is expressed."

Me: "How can you make a hole in the stone with a sewing thread?"

Him: "With the creative power of love. You, the thread, and the stone share one thing - love. In this dimension, you are One.

In that awareness, you still distinguish yourself from the stone and the thread, but also you are aware that everything is one. You know that your body or the rock are just settings that your mind has chosen from the endless possibilities of One.

You can learn to change the outcome settings of your bodily mindsets with the One.

In a dream, for example, you can do 'unreasonable' things because, in this dimension, the rules of reality are free to be as they are - a reality weher you participate in its creation."

Me: "These things you tell me sound like fairy tales to me/us in my world. We think these fairy tales are just fairy tales ... and anyone who wants to believe in this world of fantasy is trying to escape reality ..."

Him: "Yes, you may think so as you grow older. But it is the broad reality, and only the fear of love translates it into doubt and delusion and blocks awareness of the more comprehensive reality.

Ultimately, humanity will realize that the basis of reality is not as defined and limited as you once thought.

Me: "So, what will change?"

Him: "Man will begin to realize the "energy" that can affect and change things in the physical world. When one realizes that the basis of reality is actually free of laws and definitions, and that the basic energy that sustains it is only love. Fear will not interfere with that love to materialize and the reality of your world will change accordingly.

Every person will understand that he is free and responsible for the reality he experiences because he participates in it."

Me: "You said energy, what is that energy?"

Him: "As I said, it's a tremendous energy of love that exists in everything, even in solid material; in fact, it's the energy that also gives things their physical existence.

Every cell in your body contains this energy, in your concepts, you will call it - nuclear power.

One of the manifestations of this energy is the nuclear explosion.

That enormous energy that can erase entire cities in seconds - is just one of its physical expressions. Nuclear power is the energy of love. Love is like the glue that holds things together, which in this case is destructively released."

Me: "Please clarify the relationship between the nuclear bomb and love?"

Him: "These are different expressions of the same energy.

Nuclear energy is basically the energy that holds the parts of matter together, it's the power that holds and sustains your physical world base.

Here comes your freedom of choice and how to use this tremendous energy, you can use it to destroy or to create a new life. The ability of consciousness to change reality in a positive and controlled way is like the strength of the nuclear bomb to change the earth.

This mighty power already exists in every person and grain of sand ... and within your consciousness itself. Unlike a grain of sand, the combination of such power with the consciousness that exists in human, allows anyone to change the face of their reality.

Now I will tell you something that will probably sound strange to you: the practical meaning of that ability that exists in human consciousness: The reality - only one, only you can change it."

Me: "Me?"

Him: "Yes, only you, because the entire reality is interwoven and united within you. Your consciousness is capable of creating or choosing to change reality. Reality depends entirely on you."

Me: "Only I have this ability?"

Him: "No. It exists in everyone, in every person. Anyone can bring paradise into their reality; in fact, any person can create this reality for everyone."

Me: "How can that be? Do I set reality for others?"

Him: "Yes."

Me: "But if I set the reality for others, and anyone can do it, then they can determine my reality too... So, who is the determinant?

Him: "Everyone determines it.

You can experience it, but not understand it.

When I say you can create your reality, I mean that you can create reality for you, and that reality, like everything else, is not only yours. However, you make changes if you want.

You could say that the ONE gave you the ability to create your own reality with everyone else.

The essential natural need within you is to live and to be happy or blissful. The need for happiness will lead you to understand and learn how to change your reality.

Some can translate this need, and achieve something… world peace or wealth, power, love, control, connection to nature, sex, saving the world and the animals, spiritual salvation, Or the coming of the Messiah. But everyone longs for their understanding of achieving happiness. The same thing in different ways."

Me: "Salvation? - Could there be a Messiah to redeem humanity?"

He looked into my eyes and smiled without moving his lips.

Him: "Yes, this also can exist if you choose it, but he will have to come by you! And through you. Every person is the ONE, and only ONE person can bring salvation to the reality he is experiencing."

Me: "What do you mean? How can that happen?"

Him: "Try to think beyond the separation way you normally think.

When everyone is connected to the One, every person is also the entire world! That is the practical meaning of Oneness and your freedom of choice within it! Every person influences and participates in the creation of the whole world and experiences it together.

No matter who or what the Messiah will be, there will be salvation in that reality for everyone."

Me: "I'm not sure I understood ..."

Him: "... what you call the Messiah, can, but doesn't have to be a person who will solve all the problems and hence bring salvation. Everyone is responsible for the state of his world."

Me: "You're saying that the whole reality is in my consciousness, that I'm inventing it, and everything that happens in it - depends only on me?"

Him: "Here you are, again, drifting to the understanding of what I'm saying through your dual vision - black or white.

The whole reality is not only in your consciousness, as far as you are concerned, it is only what your consciousness is capable of. And secondly, you don't make it up. But you can choose from many options of reality that creation allows. Either the ways of happiness or even redemption can become possible.

At the present stage of your existence, you are in a specific developmental process of your consciousness, in conjunction with the physical dimension. Therefore, you are in a physical body. The method of this development requires a physical restriction to that perpetual experience.

Your self-consciousness development is happening, thanks to this limitation, the limitation of its ability in the physical body.

This restriction exists for a specific purpose. That man would create, with/through the physical body, the same conditions in his consciousness for that blissful experience.

The initial need or purpose of your existence in the body is for the development of physical consciousness. The effort of achieving bliss in the physical world with the help of the physical body - is one of the tools to achieve this purpose."

Me: "How is this process going on?"

Him: "All of the conditions that correspond to the experiences of bliss are based on one thing, and expressed many ways of touch and connection.

Or in your words – love. Love, but not only as an emotion."

Me: "How can this bliss be achieved?"

Him: "Your soul is the closest 'other' place to your physical recognition of yourself, and it is also where there is no limit for that, the soul is always in contact with the Creator, the infinite ONE, and your soul is a part of it.

The most significant amount of happiness and bliss you can have is through contact with your soul, when your body or physical consciousness makes contact with your soul.

To create such a state of conscious connection between the body and the soul, in physical terms, is not an easy job in your world. It is like a combination of oil and water. Opposites that exist together without one eliminating the other."

Me: "How can this be done?"

Him: "The contact between them can be created through a resonant connection, a similarity like in the frequency of them.

Your soul is conscious of your body, aware of it, loving, and responsible for its existence. She receives her liveliness from creation and carries it to the body.

The body works differently; it belongs to the physical world, and its defined needs are more self-centered.

If your physical body awareness finds a way to notice your soul, to vibrate at the same frequency, you will resonate with her; the resonance will form an infusion between your infinite soul and you.

The feeling of bliss that will be felt in your physical consciousness will be the affirmation of your consciousness for a connection made with the soul."

I felt the need to remember this understanding that the visitor now gave me:

Me: "Do you think I'll remember what you told me just now? Or will I assume that everything we are experiencing now is a dream?"

Him: "It can be your choice. If you will love yourself (not the ego perspective of you) enough to connect with your soul, you will also understand how you came here.

You will accept that this world is just as real as your world, and as you grow older, you may know how to unite them together. "

That was the communication between the visitor and myself that came to me at once, while I was sitting silently in the process of regression with Jacob.

I am now still with my eyes closed; the memory of the encounter with the visitor when I was 3 years old is over. I couldn't tell Jacob anything about that communication. It felt like only a moment since I said to Jacob that I had entered the visitor's world and we were walking together on the beach.

Jacob: "Can you draw me the world that you see?"

Me: "Yes."

Jacob brought me a white sheet and a pencil, and I slowly opened my eyes, drawing the picture I saw, the beach, me and him walking hand in hand, the huge rocks in the distance were transparent in some places and formed cliffs high up in the distance. Some of the rocks contained structures that were made of the same material as the rocks, some of which had smooth and transparent domes that covered them.

My hands trembled as I drew. My eyes continued to tear, and I was both excited and embarrassed.

When I sketched the transparent domes over the structures, I was suddenly struck by the realization that many of the paintings which I had painted over the years had almost the same transparent dome and a black space above.

The regression was over, and I went to wash my face. When I returned, I heard Jacob and Doron talking about the hypnotic regression. I didn't really listen; I was overwhelmed by the memory.

I apologized for not being able to stay and said goodbye to them.

Figure 2 Going for the One, Yossi Ronen, oil on canvas.

"You are not a drop in the ocean. You are the entire ocean in a drop"

--Rumi

Eleven

Parallels Between Human Knowledge and the Visitor's Perception

During the time since the contact, many changes in my perception of reality have followed which led me to reconsider my interests. My childhood desire and curiosity to understand reality and learn about it only through the scientific conception have changed and I have now expanded beyond that. My experience in the presence of the visitors has acted as a kind of temporary enlightenment in an environment that has always been dark for me.

This is similar to a baby who is born and always lives only in the same dark room without knowing all his life that the room is actually dark. Only after the light in the room turns on, and he can see the surroundings does he realize that there is such a possibility. I knew that the same light that was on for a moment, was not from a source that was external to me, it was not that the visitors turned on the light for me. Something in my consciousness that had always been there, and had not been known to me until then, was abruptly activated.

The desire to understand what has changed in my awareness at those moments led me to explore my present understanding of perception and consciousness. I look for a similar way of perception I had with the visitors as knowledge. My experience of the ONE, as the main concept I felt during my encounter, was the guide and the goal for that search. I experienced the ONE "language" and knew I would recognize it if I came upon it in future research.

Something with a similar understanding.

After several years of searching for spiritual works and ancient knowledge, I found something that exhibited very similar patterns and meanings to my experience, it came from an unexpected place, a place I did not expect to contain something close to the ONE experience - the Bible.

Since I was born a Jewish man in Israel, I learned the Bible in elementary school. The contact with the visitors did not remind me of anything I had learned.

It all started randomly, talking to my dad one evening when he wasn't feeling well (he was in the early stages of Alzheimer's disease) and he retired to bed earlier than usual. I went into his room to make sure he was okay and I saw him mutter something with closed eyes.

I asked him what he was saying, and he replied: "Hear O Israel the Lord our God the Lord is One."

And he continued, asking me to say this verse every night before I fell asleep.

It amazed me that my non-religious father uttered these words!

That verse was already familiar to me. I always understood it only as a sentence that defines monotheism - the belief in one god instead of many. One as an expression of quantity and that's it.

But this time I felt in this verse, another feeling that comes with a strange thought; could the primary intent of this sentence be in the word ONE?

Could it be that its real intention related to that ONE I experienced with the visitors? Could it be that the deeper intent of this statement is related to the evolution of consciousness itself? Is it a kind of mantra for practicing the awareness that all is ONE?

At first, the very thought of a connection between any religion and the visitors or the ONE light I experienced seemed ridiculous to me.

Out of curiosity, I searched the Bible to see if there was a connection there, between the belief in the Creator and the word One. I saw that it was explicitly stated - that in the future, the Creator's name will be - ONE.

It also said, as part of a prophecy about that day, that in terms of the Torah, this is the most important time for humanity, the day of salvation, the day when the consciousness of mankind will arise:

"...In that day shall the Lord be One and His name One"
(cf. Sifrei Devarim 31:10)

An interpretation of this sentence:

"The verse expresses the purpose of the world. The purpose of creation, which is to discover the oneness of the Creator in the earthly world, which also has darkness and evil. That everything in the world is part of the Creator's appearance in the world. Therefore, there is no

contradiction between Holy and non-Holy, between material and spirit and between body and soul."
--Michael Ezra

I was surprised to read that the meaning of this essential Bible sentence, indeed, is related to the evolution of our consciousness. The statement relates that the purpose of creation is to lead to a change in our perception of consciousness. Realizing the manifestation of the ONE in the world that is dually perceived by us.

On further examination, I saw that even according to the Christian belief - saying this sentence, is the first and most important of all:

The Greatest Commandment (Mark 12)

28. One of the teachers of the law came and heard them debating. Noticing that Jesus had given them a good answer, he asked him, 'Of all the commandments, which is the most important?'

29. 'The most important one,' answered Jesus, is this: 'Hear, O Israel, The Lord our God, the Lord is One'.

30. 'Love the Lord your God with all your heart and with all your soul and with all your mind and with all your strength.'

31. The second is this: 'Love your neighbor as yourself.'[g] There is no commandment greater than these."

Here, I could no longer ignore the clear resemblance to the basic perception of the visitors - the knowledge that everything is ONE, and the feeling of love is the tool and consciousness is the way to experience it.

In the Islam faith, I found the same:
(Wikipedia – Tawhid)

***Tawhid** is the religion's central and single most important concept, upon which a Muslim's entire faith rests. It unequivocally holds that God is **One** (Al-ʾAḥad) and Single (Al-Wāḥid).[6][7]*

I cannot say that I clearly understand the connection between the visitors and the Bible verses, but I also cannot ignore the connection between what is written there, and what I experienced in meeting them.

However, I do not mean that I understood from the visitors that the Bible or other spiritual conceptions are closer than others. In our communication, there has never been any reference to any human knowledge, religion, faith, or belief.

I believe they leave us with the ways we can choose to receive and create the meaning that comes from conversing with them.

One of the closest explanations that I acquired that relates to the visitors' perception, I found in Genesis.

A few words as an introduction:

According to my experience, the fundamental difference between the visitors' experience of reality, and ours is their ability to experience differentiation indiscriminately.

When they briefly allowed me to see and experience reality as they did, it was the most powerful experience and revelation I ever had.

In those moments, one actually sees the unity through the bond between the layers in our reality.

Two days after the visitors disappeared, that direct experience of Oneness I felt, also disappeared. I returned to normal consciousness and the feelings remained only as wonderful memories.

What was going on in my mind during those moments that made this experience possible? How is it possible, if only for a short time, to experience reality in such a way? Where is the door within us, that separates and/or connects that wide awareness with ordinary consciousness?

I believe that in the story of Adam and Eve in paradise, there is a description of such a door; it is called the tree of the knowledge of good and evil.

Twelve

Lost Paradise the Journey of Consciousness

According to the Bible story, the origin of all mankind - the first human, was created as a complete meshing of the contradictory formations of matter and spirit.

Man's physical body was created from matter, and his soul from God:

"And the LORD God formed man of the dust of the ground, and breathed into his nostrils the breath of life, and man became a living soul."

Man is created as the perfection of a connection between essences that contradict each other. He is the manifestation of the full connection of both, - his limited material body with the living soul, which is the limitless breadth of the Creator itself. Man is the expression and existence of those opposites that come together, matter and spirit, light and darkness, good and evil - when they become one.

The full and complete connection to one of these opposites has a consequence - if we connect the light with darkness, we will not receive half-light and half-darkness, we will receive light. This is like a light bulb lit in a dark room.

The full connection to the One between the spirit and the body in man expresses the spirit even in the material body made of dust.

This is how the Creator brings his spirit and love within the material world, - through us.

Adam and Eve - the source of all humanity, were in such a state of ONE- with each other and with reality altogether - like being together in heaven.

Their consciousness was interconnected and flowed together with the Creator, which is love.

This is how the first man with consciousness in heaven is described in the Kabbalah:

"And supreme angels rejoiced before him. And he understood supreme wisdom more than supreme angels. He looked at all. And he understood and knew his creator more than all the rest of the world ..."

In this way, when matter merges with spirit, and body merges with soul, consciousness is the mediator that connects between them. Man has his special potentiality, - to be responsible for his state of consciousness.

In doing so, the individual is distinguished from a creature programmed with a particular behavior.

Man was given the opportunity to choose for himself where to direct his consciousness which mediated between his body and soul; he was given the freedom of choice.

In heaven, Adam and Eve experienced reality through their complete consciousness - they felt their soul and body alike, as one. This is the paradise experience.

And the Creator warned them:

"You may freely eat of every tree of the garden; but of the tree of the knowledge of good and evil you shall not eat, for in the day that you eat of it you shall die."

Also:

"the serpent said to the woman, "You will not die;
for God knows that when you eat of it your eyes will
be opened, and you will be like God, knowing good and
evil."

The snake said – you will not die as God says. In fact, you will be as smart as God, knowing good and bad. The snake seemed to know what they wanted the most: they wanted to be like the Creator who gave them their lives.

Until then, they got everything from Him. But they also wanted to give, like Him, to distinguish between good and evil, like Him to shine in the darkness, create, give birth, and give life, like Him to give love.

Adam and Eve were aware of the freedom of choice they received and nourished themselves from the fruits of the tree of knowledge.

The tree of knowledge of good and evil, as its name stated, had knowledge of the difference and judgment between things. It was **separating** the good from the evil that is the whole of the ONE.

But after eating from the fruit, something happened to them; their complete consciousness had not yet experienced the difference between good and evil, and so they could not have and understand this and remain intact.

For them, eating from the fruit, had a consequence: The distinction between good and evil, in their consciousness, now became a separation between them.

In their consciousness, the view of separation was born.

All the objective reality that use to be ONE for them, seemed split from then on. Part of it looked good, and part was bad. The good had a borderline, a certain definition in space and time. On the other side of the good borderline, the evil was revealed, - defined and held separately.[2]

Their consciousness could not contain the knowledge of the good and evil duality and still see it as complete or as one whole entity.

A split inside the consciousness was born, and with it, for the first time, the fear:

---

[2] The Hebrew word "bad", is from the same root of the concept of what is not connected to its source well enough, what is about to break up and fall from his source.

"I heard the sound of you in the garden, and I was afraid because I was naked, and I hid myself."

The love and Oneness with the Creator (their "mother and father"), was then split by the fear of Him. He was suddenly experienced as separate from them.

Their consciousness that was split into good and evil, gave birth to fear and distance from their Creator. They had only known love from him. Fear of their source and all the reality around them, their entire world now entered. The quiet, safe, innocent, and boundless love that they had experienced until then, like a baby in his mother's womb, disappeared. The fear of love was born. Fear of the source of life, of their own souls.c

Their consciousness now separated the darkness from the light, the spirit from the material, their bodies from their soul. In their new split consciousness, their bodies were now separate, naked from their soul, definite and material.

God warned them that if they ate of the tree of good and evil - they would die, and so it happened. They created a boundary and separation between their bodies, and their infinite souls.

Through awareness of the distinct body created from the earth, they experienced the finality of matter – death.

But the soul of man, the Creator's breath, always remained as it was - endless.

Although their bodies were now limited and dead, their basic essence - the soul of man will go on and exist without boundaries. Even now, it continues to exist in the physical world through the changing body of each and every one of us.

The spark of the ONE soul now exists in all human beings, separated only by each consciousness.

After their consciousness - the tool for perceiving reality, split to the awareness of good and evil separately, all the reality they saw through that consciousness, now seemed divided through it. Now some of it looks good and some bad. Then for the first time, the fear in man was born:

"Then the man and his wife heard the sound of the LORD God as he was walking in the garden in the cool of the day, and they hid from the LORD God among the trees of the garden. 9 But the LORD God called to the man, "Where are you?"

"He answered, "I heard you in the garden, and I was afraid because I was naked; so, I hid."

Genesis 3:8-11

The first fear from the Creator, the One - was born.

As a result of the separation created in the consciousness of Adam and Eve, the fear of the One who is now separated from them is born. Fear of what was once the pure love that they knew of Him - the source of reality around them. The quiet, safe, unity existence, boundless, innocence, and love they had experienced up to that point - a paradise experience - split now into two. The fear of God now is also a fear of love. The fear of themselves. Is it our heeded deep and basic fear of the Oneness experience? Is it the same fear that fills each one of us at the crucial moment of birth? That split from the floating Oneness in the warm, nourishing, and protective womb of our mothers into this blinding world?

Is it the same fear that fills each one of us at the moment of birth into this world?

The word *space* - also means distance in between a "hole" in something. That space in the infinity of one consciousness has become a new dimension for us - the space in which we see the universe, our world - the physical dimension.

In this dimension, space exists, the physical reality and the dual laws that are familiar to our flesh; separation of place from place, between man and the other, between man and his creator, between this time and another, good and evil.

While communicating with the visitors, one discovers that one can see inwardly into the depths of oneself, experiencing one's soul, one's initial self without the usual separation of consciousness.

For a moment, one experiences the Oneness that gives happiness by being aware of it, innocence and love that is independent for itself. From here, one clearly sees that it is only him who separates and splits between yourself and the environment, and one can see that love is the basis of everything. You see the fear that separates you from your love, from your roots, from your soul, from yourself.[3]

---

[3] The root meaning of the word "Eden" in Hebrew is related to refinement. Distillation from coarse husks.

Thirteen

To See the Voices

Why does our brain know us, but we don't know it?
The brain connects the disappeared source that exists
in reality and the disappeared source that is not in
reality.
He is an average that connects the borderless with
the border.
--Meir Yanai
"Secret of the Brain"

The knowledge that my consciousness does not depend solely on my body was born as soon as I first experienced myself outside my body. I experienced clarity and a far greater understanding than I had received from my ordinary sense of seeing the world. I also had the awareness that I use my body as a vehicle.

Many who have experienced clinical death have felt a similar feeling, and a good example of this can be read in the book by Eben Alexander called, *Proof of Heaven.*

In his book, Eben testified that he lost most of his brain function which broke down as a result of an acute illness. Contrary to all predictions, he began to heal, and his mind returned to full function. As an experienced neurology specialist in the hospital, he was also able to research closely, and scientifically understand what happened to his brain.

He noticed that during the time when his brain was in its worst condition and his brainwaves ceased being recorded on the devices it was connected to, he still recognized that it was more like a dream in which his awareness continued.

Today, he says, as a result of his research, to the best of his understanding, consciousness is independent of the body and only uses the brain as a means of containing it. Moreover, consciousness can cause changes in brain structure and activity.

In the world of medicine, you can see evidence of this when, in some cases, a drug such as a placebo is used.

Placebos allow the person to influence the brain to function in a way that heals the body. Desire and belief seem capable of altering brain activity. The brain is flexible and able to reorganize itself.

We find it difficult to distinguish our consciousness from brain activity. But perhaps the way to recognize it is simple: we know that our thinking is done in the brain, but the choice of what we think is related to our consciousness.

Human culture from ancient times to the present day has been curious as to what consciousness is, and the mystery surrounding it is still unresolved, even though consciousness is the most fundamental source that exists in us. Science today still cannot answer this question.

The brain is, in fact, the physical tool that we experience through physical reality and thinking. And therefore, its structure directly influences and determines the nature of experienced reality.

One example is that our brains are designed to absorb and translate only a specific spectrum of colors out of the much greater variety that exists in nature. In the same regard, our hearing and all other sensory data received by the brain, we can only perceive a small fraction of what our cameras and even animals can pick up. *

In the same way, even with the one broad reality we exist in and are part of, our brain translates, differentiates, separates, and experiences it in a dual way.

During my meeting with the visitors and for a while afterward, I experienced my surrounding reality differently.

When I tried to understand what had changed inside of me after my contact, I noticed that my senses were acting differently. After my communication with the visitors, for a few hours, I had the ability to hear what I saw and see what I was hearing.

Years later, I read about a similar phenomenon. It's called synesthesia.[4]

Over time, I have found that this phenomenon is common among those who have experienced a meeting with visitors, some of them (like me) only experience the synesthesia as a temporary side effect.

---

[4] Synesthesia is a perceptual phenomenon in which stimulation of one sensory or cognitive pathway leads to involuntary experiences in a second sensory or cognitive pathway.

There is an interesting verse from the Bible, and it is perhaps related to this occurrence. This phenomenon had happened to hundreds of thousands of people, at the time of revelation on Mount Sinai:

"And all the people perceived (in Hebrew – see) the thundering and the lightning, and the voice of the horn, and the mountain smoking; and when the people saw it, they trembled, and stood afar off."

The Ramchal (biblical commentator) wrote about seeing the voices and interpreted it as follows:

"And this is called the vision of the soul, which is not the vision of the body, and not the vision of the eyes."

Our brain seems to be far more flexible and resilient than we know and can significantly change how we perceive reality.

Fourteen

Telepathy and the Connection to One

When the visitors allowed me to telepathically connect with them, I was also connected to the consciousness of the other visitors in the room; they could also feel my consciousness, we were all connected.

This was a similar experience as to when my five senses worked cohesively for a while, through synesthesia, even after my contact.

An interesting explanation of the phenomenon in which each part is distinct from the whole – but also contains the whole, I discovered a few years later in Michael Talbot's amazing book, *The Holographic Universe*.

The scientific foundation of the book relies on the studies of the eminent theoretical physicist, David Bohm, and the brain researcher Karl Pribram.

In today's scientific world, the holographic principle is considered to be the foundation of many of the leading theories that explain not only the physical structure of reality, but the activity of the brain, consciousness, and the phenomena associated with it.

The author chose the name "holographic universe" (the term used by many scientists now) because of the similarity to the structure of the holographic image.

One of the aspects of a holographic image occurs if you divide it into parts, and every part of it, even the smallest - will contain the appearance of the complete image.

This book offers an understanding that every particle in the universe contains the information of the entire universe. Or as written in the book:

"Bohm believes the same is true at our own level of existence. Space is not empty. It is full, a plenum as opposed to a vacuum, and is the ground for the existence of everything, including ourselves. The universe is not separate from this cosmic sea of energy, it is a ripple on

its surface, a comparatively small 'pattern of excitation'
in the midst of an unimaginably vast ocean."
– MICHAEL TALBOT
The Holographic Universe

Our conflict or difficulty in understanding this concept is due to the fact that there is really **no separation between consciousness and the brain - only difference**.

The consciousness that we experience, even if it is not a product of the brain, is ultimately experienced through the brain and its system of senses.

In other terms, we think and talk through our physical brain, it is cognitively difficult to understand how differentiation is possible without separation.

However, our usual, dual method of perception is essential to our normal day-to-day functioning.

At present, the ability to feel or to be aware of our consciousness beyond the dual conception of the brain usually occurs and is experienced only in exceptional cases such as leaving the body, at clinical death, in deep meditation, because of a head injury or an accident, and the like.

All of these actually silence or weaken the normal activity of the brain, to the point where we sometimes experience recognition beyond the cognitive control of the brain, beyond its normal dualistic separating concept.

The duality of the brain is also seen in that the brain is simply divided into two distinct parts, the right hemisphere, and the left hemisphere. The right is responsible for emotion, intuition, empathy, and creativity, and the left hemisphere is responsible for logic, language, rational, and analytical thinking.

It also seems that the right side of the brain elicits a wider scope of thinking before the left side selects, makes a preference, and decides to act in a certain way.

Even in meditation practice, in order to achieve the inner peace that allows connection to one's higher consciousness, some practitioner work is required to quiet the thoughts, in fact, a silencing of the left "chattering" side of the brain. This side is also where our ego experience lives, (as opposed to the authentic self) and can often interfere with the functioning of the two lobes of the brain.

Our ability to connect to the "external" consciousness exists within us as a great potential, except that this ability must pass through the mediation of our brain.

Therefore, this possibility could seem difficult and blocked at times.

I believe that removing this block is possible by connecting the different parts of the brain and not strengthening or silencing part of it.

Each of us can influence our own brain activity to allow this, and I believe that realizing and using this potential is critical for us.

I believe that freeing us from this block is also related to the purpose of the visitor's contact with us from ancient times to the present.

Figure 3 The Crystal, Yossi Ronen, oil on canvas.

Fifteen

The One Dimension Theory

When the visitors explained to me where they came from, I experienced their answer in a more abstract, intuitive way. The closest literal translation for me was that they came from a different dimension.[5]

What exactly did they mean by this?

---

[5] The use I make of the word "dimension," here is not linked only to its customary meaning, dimension, being a mathematical space. It includes the meaning of a non-physical essence, which is not limited to the laws of physics known to us.

It took time for me to realize that during the meeting itself, I did not understand that they were showing me the way they move into that other dimension. I think they did that travel, through pure use of their consciousness ability.

As I mentioned before, the visitors have made it clear that they can appear to us with a physical body, but that is not their only essence. They know how to move between dimensions, between the one we know as the physical, and another dimension.

As I described in the first chapter, when the visitors decided to stop the meeting and disappeared from my eyes, they walked away to the edge of the room, stood in a circle, clasped their hands and began to walk and move around the center of it. The movement of the rotation grew so much that it became a circle that looked like a white light that was moving at a tremendous speed, the white rotating circle getting smaller and smaller and move to its center until it became so tiny it disappeared from my eyes.

From my point of view that is how they moved towards that other dimension. I believe that Their consciousness ability allowed them to move and transform themselves into what is physically visible to us as a very tiny point in space.

In the world of physics, the tiniest space is the subatomic or the quantum field.

If I understood correctly, the point or the gate of transition from our physical space to that other dimension is through that very small physical point in space. a point in space that is much smaller than we can see. Perhaps it is more accurate to say that this is such a small point that further beyond it, our current meaning of space and time no longer exists or is relevant.

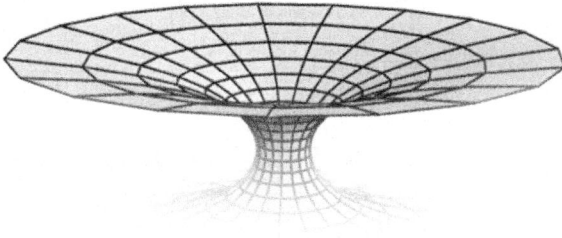

*Figure 4: The shortest measurable physical length is about 1.62 x 10 -35, a very small number... (and it is the minimum length unit of the black hole radius according to the uncertainty principle.) * see Planck length*

Even if we try to understand where or what is the Length of the point in time, that we call - the present, we will get the same result. If the past tense is unrealistic because it does not already exist, and the future tense is unrealistic because it does not exist yet, how long is the present?

A small point in time? infinitely small? without a limit?

What happens to time beyond this point? No time? One time?

This means that this is the point of transition, and the connection between the material world in time - and the minuscule, limitless, quantum world. And as well as the point of the connection to the different physical laws that operate there. Different laws of nature rule this invisible, quantum reality – which is the basis of our entire physical world. In my point of view, the gateway to this other dimension is a place where time and space are so small that they are not a physical space in the way we know and perceive it.

In my understanding, this is the gate for the ONE dimension, a dimension in which time is not linear, just as the way the visitors perceive it to be.

The One dimension is here and now - all around us. Since it is not divided into linear time or space, it is everywhere, and at all times. It is the basis of every small particle in our reality.

This fact also may explain the nature of the spirit world, the essence, and the "elusive" nature of our consciousness.

It explains why quantum size substance can be affected by our consciousness - our attention, emotions, and desire. In my opinion, those experiments in quantum space which prove that our consciousness affects quantum size matter, actually show that our awareness and quantum size overlap and belong to the same dimension, this is why they interact.

We can understand how it is that our consciousness interacts with the quantum space of every physical cell in us, in our brain activity. we can understand how our thoughts can directly affect the body. Those thoughts are part of the basic quantum wave activity of our brain.

Another dimension is not in a different physical place but contains it. It is here exactly where we are, but on a level that our ordinary consciousness is not yet aware of. The one dimension contains the familiar reality of our physical dimension.

When our mindfulness goes beyond its usual place of our physical dimensional reality, we may get a glimpse of the One dimension.

As we return to normal recognition with a memory of clinical death, for example, we can retain the remember of this other dimension. But in a normal sense of waking reality, it is difficult for us to understand what remains in us as a memory of the visit to this alternate, vast dimension.

It challenges our dualistic logical thinking, and I believe that this is also why our ordinary consciousness at this point prevents us from being fully exposed to this infinite wealth. We are not yet ready for it. We still do not know how to move our consciousness within the one dimension as the visitors do, and we Don't even know how to translate and contain it as memory. It is difficult for us to accept that what we remember is just a translation of a visit to a dimension where the laws of reality are completely different. But, because we are sometimes allowed a glimpse, and can retain a memory of visiting this area, we know that we can experience it, and that ability can evolve!

There seems to be a connection between our range of special experiences in that "other" dimension – such as in dreams, telepathy, remote viewing, out-of-body experiences, the clinical death experience, meeting with the visitors, inspiration, and many more. These are glimpses into the same "place": the ONE dimension.

Sixteen

Automatic Writing Inseparable Differentiation and Uniqueness of the One

A distinction without separation is also individualism that does not negate and contradict the other.

Your fear of losing self- definition in life to the other, or in meeting us, is a natural consequence of your approach to reality today.

This approach can change and indeed will change, and the reason is simple; since there are signs that you are already on the way to the consciousness of One, you will discover through the same process that you will realize that the Oneness we aspire to can only be realized by the unique discovery and expression of the individual in it. The personal discovery of uniqueness in each one will allow everyone's experience of the Oneness.

Thanks to the individual's self-recognition of his unique self - it is his self that is distinct from the others, the deep recognition and connection to the other will be possible. Therefore, one can see that in the end, there is not much chance of further development of the phenomena of separation and control in human society as they exist today.

When you become acquainted with the multidimensional law that requires direction and personal need for each to expand in his or her own way, phenomena such as the desire to control or abolish the other will become known as self-destruction.

Seventeen

The Original Role of Man and The Influence of Human Consciousness on The Environment

Just before the end of the face-to-face contact, the visitors conveyed to me their message about the alarming state of the earth.

Over the years, I have seen that the visitors share this same message to almost everyone they contact.

The meaning of the message is received in different ways but it is the same message; the earth, and we, are in danger.

In my personal experience of receiving this information, I had a vision of the catastrophe, the huge fire resembling a fire that erupts after a nuclear explosion, approaching and basically burning everything in its path.

Along with these pictures, I experienced another layer, an emotional layer of responsibility for what could happen. The responsibility which was beyond the destruction in the ecological sense and environmental consideration.

The responsibility was for life itself, for those innocent cows I saw burning, while alive, in front of my eyes. The look in their eyes of the cows a moment before the fire reached them, did not contain anger, guilt, or terror. They were calm because they assumed that we would protect them.

The feeling of pain I felt in those moments did not go away, even after all the years that had passed. This feeling pushed me to try to understand more deeply why it was so important for these gentle and loving visitors to show me these images that evoked in me such a deep sense of emotional pain, sorrow, and the sense of responsibility for that destruction.

Through other means of communication between us, including automatic writing, the purpose of this feeling became clear. This responsibility for Earth's condition comes from the direct connection between earth and our state of consciousness.

In fact, the purpose of this prophecy to me and to many others who have experienced a similar one is to awaken our awareness of that.

Human's influence on earth through climate change is the noticeable result of our deeper influence, an effect that is not visible and is directly related to our state of understanding.

There seems to be a field of consciousness common to us and to the nature around us where we have a significant influence on it.

Over time, I found that there is a similar concept in the Torah.

According to the Torah, in Genesis, the original role of man given to him by the Creator was to preserve nature and determine its essence:

"And the LORD God took the man, and put him into the garden of Eden to dress it and to keep it."

Genesis 2: 15

"And out of the ground the LORD God formed every beast of the field and every fowl of the air, and brought them unto the man to see what he would call them; and whatsoever the man would call every living creature, that was to be the name thereof."

Genesis 2:19

Beyond working and preserving nature in heaven, the Creator also gave man the role of determining the names of the animals. In doing so, the Creator had actually enabled man to participate in the creation of life in nature and to define the unique essence of each.

In the Torah (the first five books of the Hebrew Bible), there are many examples that clarify the profound importance of the name given to man and every other entity and its influence. For example, the Creator changes Abram's name to Abraham, and in Jacob's encounter with an angel, Jacob receives a new name for himself, Israel.[6]

This ability is inherent in a human being because of his unique essence which is the creator's soul, fully

---

[6] In the Midrash, commentary on the Hebrew scriptures, it is explained that the Creator chose to give man the role of giving the names because he was better suited to it than the beings who were in a spiritual realm higher than him, like the angels. For only man could correctly link the physical being of animals to their essence as the Creator intended when he created them. (Midrash Genesis, chapter 4)

combined with his physical body here on earth. In fact, man was given the role of being the bridge and mediator between the Creator and creation, between the spirit and the material world.

It is still difficult for us to digest and accept the deep meaning of this role. At this stage, we are just facing the fact that the earth is in danger due to man's misbehavior with nature and the destruction of its balance.

The new study by modern science makes it clear that human consciousness affects matter, but this understanding has not yet been fully accepted. Most quantum physics researchers prefer not to consider its deep meaning, its broad meaning beyond the precise computational capability it provides.

The understanding that our awareness influences matter shows us that there is a direct connection between man and nature and it is much deeper than what we currently accept.

Man's state of consciousness in heaven before eating the fruit of the tree of knowledge of good and evil was different – an entire consciousness full of love.

When man was given the job of preserving and working with nature, meditating, through his body, between the spirit of creation and material world, naming details in creation, he actually participated in determining the nature of every plant and animal in it. Accordingly, human consciousness that was full also affected the consciousness of animals in the world. In heaven, both humans and animals did not eat the flesh of another mammal.

When man has "fallen" from heaven, it is, in fact, his consciousness that has fallen. At the same time, the reality that he is experiencing has "fallen."

Today humans and animals eat one another's flesh.

Since the level of consciousness of nature on earth is intertwined and even dependent on that of man, as soon as man's awareness is transformed and realized in its entirety, the entire consciousness of nature, including the animals, will change with it.

Here is what the prophet Isaiah said about the days when human consciousness will return to its fullness and fulfill its purpose:

This prophecy is titled - *The End of Days Prophecy*:

"The wolf also shall dwell with the lamb, and the leopard shall lie down with the kid; and the calf and the young lion and the fatling together, and a little child shall lead them.

And the cow and the bear shall feed; their young ones shall lie down together: and the lion shall eat straw like the ox.

And the sucking child shall play on the hole of the asp, and the weaned child shall put his hand on the cockatrice' den.

They shall not hurt nor destroy in all my holy mountain: for the earth shall be full of the knowledge of the LORD, as the waters cover the sea."

In light of the similar understanding I have gained from the visitors and also in the face of the new revelations of modern science, I believe that this prophecy was not merely a parable or a legend.

Human consciousness affects the "consciousness" of nature, it is an integral part of it, so this prophecy can indeed be fulfilled as it is written.

Epilogue

Meeting with the visitors has radically changed my perception of life. Besides the shock of meeting them, what I experienced when I was able to connect with their wider consciousness was more palpable to me than anything I had ever before encountered. The experience included the recognition of the undefined *One* light, no matter what concept I use to describe this experience - "God," "Nature," "Supreme Power," "Creator of Reality." These are all different translations of the same experience, the source of existence.

From the moment I experienced this feeling, I have never forgotten it. It was an awe-inspiring moment and brought blissfulness in my life so far.

This feeling also came from knowing our existence is an integral part of our conscious creation, that our existence is not random. There is a purpose for our world and our existence. It may be that the clear understanding of what surrounds us is love, which is ultimately the essence that leads the course of our world affairs for better or worse.

Another layer to this blissfulness is the sense of privilege and knowing that we humans can at any moment participate in the creation of ourselves with a purpose. With every breath, one can consciously connect with the same love and participate in the creation and the dissemination of this light to places still lacking it.

You can experience the inner affirmation that you are headed in the right direction – going for the Oneness experience.

Our relationships with one another are a bridge to everything that one maintains, so this place is a person's place of connection with the entire realm of reality - with every other person, animal, plant, entity, place, or time.

When one understands and accepts that, through his consciousness, he is already connected to the One, he can affirm and allow himself the love, happiness, and healing capabilities that exist within him.

Fear will fade when we discover together, the source and purpose of our existence, simple love.

Simplicity rests in Oneness.

--- There is no end ---

Appendix

Prof. John Mack's Study

In researching numerous encounters between people and the visitors in recent years, I see that much information has been published. I noticed that these other ETs think and feel the same as what I experienced. Today, a large part of the human population is beginning to realize that it is happening, but for the most part, it is difficult to understand what <u>it</u> is.

In recent years, psychological tests and research have been conducted on the subject.

Important research was done by Professor John Mack and written in his book, *Abduction*.

John Mack was a professor and head of psychiatry at Harvard Medical School, Cambridge Hospital, and was the founder and superintendent of the Center for Psychology and Social Change in the United States.

His previous book, *A Prince of our Disorder*, written on psychiatry, was published in 1976 and won the Pulitzer Prize.

Dr. Mack described how, after his 40 years of working in the field of psychiatry, three patients who, through his treatment of hypnotic regression, were first discovered to have met, or been abducted by extraterrestrials, or as I call them "visitors."

Mack relates that because of apparent similarities between the descriptions of his three patients, who had no connection, he decided to bring them together to be present at a meeting.

At this meeting, he came to know in a way that, as far as he was concerned, left no doubt that the three of them had a robust and unusual experience in their lives.

It was a similar experience to others and one that did not amount to just their inner world.

With interest and curiosity about this, he asked his colleagues to refer patients to him who claimed to have met with the visitors. In a few months, dozens of people were examined by John Mack. At that point, he already realized that the phenomenon of meeting the visitors was much broader than what he once thought. As a result of getting to know his patients, he knew that he had come into contact with an extraordinary and significant phenomenon that was contacting humanity.

ONE

For about three years, he researched and studied the subject in-depth, and his medical research on the subject concluded in the writing of many books.

Immediately after the first book was published, it was enthusiastically received around the world. On the other hand, Mack was also harshly attacked by the academic establishment in the U.S. and the world for what was said in this book.

They criticized the fact that a world-renowned psychiatry professor, who taught at the great universities in the world, published a book about his conclusions on such a subject. He also dared to argue that all of humanity faced an important phenomenon on a historical scale, which it must study, and take seriously and responsibly.

After the controversies subsided, John eventually received approval from Harvard University to publish the results of his research.

I chose to bring here quotes from the book, some by John Mack and some by his patients:

Many of the experiencers report that the extraterrestrial (guests) themselves say that humanity is not ready to face their existence yet. They argue that we may aggressively

187

confront their existence as if they were enemies, as someone or something different from us, something we do not understand.

--John Mack

Some of the experiencers say that the beings do not want to make a change in our world through correction by them, but prefer the change in our consciousness that will lead us to choose a different path independently.

--John Mack

Many of the experiencers have a sense that strangers come from the "forgotten home.

--John Mack

...At the time of the encounter, you have a feeling that the cosmos itself is intelligent, the feeling of separating from everything breaks with the experience of One, which becomes essential in the development of the consciousness of meeting them ...

--From the testimony of one of the patients of John Mack

At some point, I had to deal with understanding my experience or deteriorating into a loss of sanity ...
    – Patient Joe

... I realized that we must break the barriers of fear between people and create communication lines based on love and healing ...
    --Patient Joe

Many describe that the visitors appear as part of their souls themselves ... as another dimension to reality
    --John Mack

There are experiences that describe an orgasmic sense of trance and tremendous lift ... along with a sense of openness and unity with the beings, there is a oneness feeling with the Creator.
    --John Mack

For the abducted, this experience is enlightening and colorful; they sometimes cry through these feelings because separation from this feeling is painful beyond words.
    --John Mack

Some who meet with them, are left with the feeling that this awakening in awareness, must translate into some kind of higher teaching or purpose.
--John Mack

It is an experience that is very much about expanding personal identity, far beyond its boundaries.
--John Mack

For some abductees, the guests look like messengers or angels from God, and on the other hand, to some people, they look like apostles from the devil ...
--John Mack

The difficulty in explaining what happened there, (the pairing with the beings) stems from the fact that the media and language we built are constructed to convey concepts related to the physical world, while they are from other dimensions - it happened half here and half in other dimensions ...
--Patient Sarah

They are mentally connected to each other. They seemed excited and amused ...
 – Patient Eva

Although psychoanalysis has helped a great deal in our lives and is responsible for a great deal of progress in our information about human experiences and the structure and depth of mind or consciousness - it has retained much information related to the objectivity and division of object, the one that characterizes the Western world and psychiatry. Traditionally, this state of awareness (which the abductees tell about) can be called distortion. However, from a transpersonal-interpersonal perspective, the experimenter and I (the therapist) can be part of evolution.
 --John Mack

Experiencing contact with the visitors says that while there is a slight change in recognition while communicating with them, they are sure that they are not dreaming or imagining. Even if some of them experience having been transformed into a different reality, for them, it is a reality where they feel awake but different and discover a new reality for experimentation.

--John Mack

...In many cases in the encounter, experiencers see different forms of the same extraterrestrials, and so probably the extraterrestrials themselves can change their form - disguising them as they wish for different kinds of animals or people...

--John Mack

Bibliography

Additional sources for enriching the knowledge related to the book and its subjects - at the book's website:

www.oneyossironen.com

Video conference with Grant Cameron about the book, in two parts:

part one:

https://www.youtube.com/watch?v=jl2_yFCyxDs&t=183s

part two:

https://www.youtube.com/watch?v=gnUpKyd75_0&t=85s

Chapter Four

Book: Communion: A True Story by Louis Whitley Strieber.

Chapter Six

1. Book: Varieties of Religious Experience, a Study in Human Nature | by William James.

2. Clinical death: Wikipedia:

https://en.wikipedia.org/wiki/Clinical_death

Chapter Seven

1. YouTube movie - Infinite Potential: The Life and Ideas of David Bohm:

https://www.youtube.com/watch?v=XDpurdHKpb8

2. Quantum mechanics

Wikipedia:

https://en.wikipedia.org/wiki/Quantum_mechanics

Quantum Entanglement - Wikipedia

Quantum Entanglement is a phenomenon in quantum mechanics in which the quantum states of two or more objects must always be described in relation to each other, despite the possibility that the objects are physically distant from each other (non-local behavior.) In classical physics, this can be described as a wave function that denotes the common quantum state of all parts in light-years.

The quantum intersection was demonstrated not only in space (physically distant objects) but also in time - between objects that do not exist at the same time.

3. Waves and particles - Proof of Mind Over Matter - The Double Slit Experiment - Physics, Dr. Quantum

YouTube movie -

https://www.youtube.com/watch?v=btImof4nyzo

4. Dean Radin, the experiment particle behavior also varies depending on its participant

Wikipedia: https://en.wikipedia.org/wiki/Dean_Radin

5. Nils Bohr:

"Everything, in reality, we call real, is made of things we can't say are real." Wikiquote:

https://en.wikiquote.org/wiki/Niels_Bohr

6. Fritjof Capra:

Wikipedia: https://en.wikipedia.org/wiki/Fritjof_Capra

7. Werner Heisenberg

Wikipedia:

https://en.wikipedia.org/wiki/Werner_Heisenberg

Chapter Ten

1.Nuclear energy

Wikipedia:

Nuclear energy is the energy of the atomic nucleus. The concept of energy utilization usually refers to the needs of the person. The atomic nucleus consists of protons and neutrons that are interconnected by the nuclear force. When they are separated, nuclear contact energy is released.

Chapter Thirteen

1.Meir Yanai - "Secret of the Brain"

2.Dr. Donald Huffman

Wikipedia:

https://en.wikipedia.org/wiki/Donald_Huffman

Chapter Fourteen

1.Michael Talbot's book, *The Holographic Universe*

Wikipedia: https://en.wikipedia.org/wiki/Michael_Talbot
_(author)

YouTube: Synchronicity and the Holographic Universe -
Thinking Allowed

Part 1.

https://www.youtube.com/watch?v=6rgYz_BU2Ew

Part 2.

https://www.youtube.com/watch?v=9ugQBP3NQ2g

2.Karl H. Pribram

Wikipedia:

https://en.wikipedia.org/wiki/Karl_H._Pribram

YouTube:

https://www.youtube.com/watch?v=vHpTYs6GJhQ

3.Jill Bolte Taylor

TED

My stroke of insight - the effect of paralysis on the left
side of the brain

https://www.youtube.com/watch?v=UyyjU8fzEYU&feature=youtu.be

Quantum Entanglement - Wikipedia

Quantum Entanglement is a phenomenon in quantum mechanics in which the quantum states of two or more objects must always be described in relation to each other, despite the possibility that the objects are physically distant from each other (non-local behavior.) Of classical physics, but can be described as a wave function that denotes the common quantum state of all parts in light-years.

The quantum intersection was demonstrated not only in space (physically distant objects) but also in time - between objects that do not exist at the same time.

Art and Graphics

The book cover:

- The front cover includes my drawing of one of the visitors as I saw him in the face-to-face contact.

- Arrival Logograms, as chapter titles

The film "Arrival," based on the short story "Story of Your Life" by Ted Chiang, focuses on humans trying to communicate with mysterious aliens.

YouTube: Arrival Movie's Language: Talking in Circles
https://www.youtube.com/watch?v=Qd8zT1YAUck

YouTube: Arrival: A Response to Bad Movies
YouTube:
https://www.youtube.com/watch?v=z18LY6NME1s

My artwork that is related to the encounter:
https://www.oneyossironen.com/channeling-art

Printed in Great Britain
by Amazon

63256064R00122